Practical
Pointer
Training

Practical Pointer Training

Hints on Training the Pointing Breeds of Bird Dogs

Sherman Webb

Photographs by
Bruce L. Webb

WINCHESTER PRESS

To my wife Mildred and to my sons Gary and Bruce,
who have tolerated over the years—perhaps at times
with interest—the discussion of the ever-popular
subjects of good bird dogs, and the comparison of good
and bad points of the English setter and the English
pointer.

Library of Congress Catalog Card Number: 74-21955
ISBN: 0-87691-131-9

Published by Winchester Press
460 Park Avenue, New York 10022

Printed in the United States of America

Contents

Introduction

For me, the most interesting species in the whole animal world has always been the dog, more specifically, the bird dog. Deep interest in the subject of bird dogs has driven me to try to learn all there is to know about dogs. I am still learning.

Of course, no man, during his short life span, can by his own effort and personal experience learn the many complexities of dog behavior. He must learn from the writings of knowledgeable authors with a lifetime devoted to association with dogs of varied character. He must evaluate, compare and experiment with dogs of many different temperaments. To fully understand the dog is quite an undertaking; but it is also a pleasant, absorbing experience.

To the man deeply interested in the character of bird dogs, it is difficult to sympathize with those who show a degree of interest but never bother to investigate what makes each one have like characteristics, yet also little personal traits of character which set it apart.

Certain dogs stand out in the memory. Even trainers who have handled hundreds of dogs will find that one or two of them occupy a very special niche. The dog may not have been the best-looking individual or the most stylish performer, but there will be something about the personality—perhaps sincerity, or trustworthiness—that makes that particular dog really special.

One dog that occupies that special niche for me is a little setter bitch named Sally. She has hunted about seven hundred days, and has never made a mistake intentionally. Every time I go hunting entirely for fun (instead of for training) Sally accompanies me.

The man who insists on the ultimate in style might not look twice at Sally; not that she doesn't have pleasing style when pointing birds, but her small size makes her straight-up points unimpressive. Then too, if she happens to crowd a bird and is afraid of flushing it, she just might drop on point.

Sally does not have phenomenal speed when hunting, but she paces herself, and she can hunt all day, every day. I have only ever

*To those who knew her, it is enough to say,
"This is Sally."*

punished her twice, and she has never
needed more—this statement can truthfully
be said of very few dogs. Sally will do for me.

I'll tell you what kind of dog she is. A few
years ago, I was hunting with a friend who
kept shooting birds while I was still looking
for my first. After a while I decided to try to
find better opportunities by moving off to one
side. We hadn't gone far when Sally pointed a
single bird, but at the flush all I could do was
wing-tip it. Sally was on the verge of catching
the runner when another bird flushed. She
immediately stopped to flush in fear of put-
ting up other birds, letting the cripple escape
into a dense brush pile. My friend filled his
limit while I came home with a jacket as

empty as last year's birdnest. But I liked the way my bitch worked.

I recently was using Sally as a lead dog. She pointed a single bird and the other dog either honored her or had bird scent in her nose. I wanted the honoring dog to flush the bird because I had put too much pressure on her and she was a bit bird-shy. I wanted her to regain some confidence. When I couldn't get her to flush, I picked Sally up by the hind feet, wheelbarrow fashion, and shoved her toward the bird. She became over-balanced and fell on her back. With her feet sticking up in the air, looking in the direction of the bird, she lay on her back and was still pointing. In fear of flushing the bird, she would not move to get on her feet! Gentlemen, this is stanchness.

I've started off this little book on dog training by telling you about Sally because it will give you an idea of what to expect from me. This is not a very fancy book because I'm not a very fancy person. Sally is my kind of dog. She's no field-trial hotshot, and no bench champion, but she's my idea of what a shooting dog should be.

If that's not what you're looking for, perhaps you shouldn't read any further. But then again, perhaps you should. Because I've had a lot of other dogs, and tried a lot of different training methods, and this experience just might be worth something to you, even if your training goals are different from mine. In any case, I can promise you that the methods described in this book have stood the test of time.

Although not often admitted, it is obvious that the vast majority of dog owners are too willing to ignore faults; to leave their dogs without the necessary guiding hand; to let them live out their lives without learning anything, without fulfilling their potentialities.

It is also obvious that the dog, like the child, is born with little knowledge but with great aptitude for learning. Unlike the child, the dog must cram his learning into two years at the most; the child learns (hopefully), if he's lucky, all his life. In order to learn the dog must attend some sort of school, and you, his owner, must be his teacher. He looks to you for his every need, including affection. The dog must respect your knowledge while he pursues the course of learning. How can you, the teacher, gain the necessary knowledge to be his teacher without first learning what you must teach him?

In this modern age, specialization is everything. A good bird dog must be a specialist, too; he must excel in his trade, which is handling game birds. He has the necessary potential to handle upland game birds better than any other breed of dog. If the specialist does not perform to this standard he is not worthy of the distinction bestowed upon him. Far too few are required to reach their peak of potential, or have the opportunity to reach it.

A bird dog trainer must also be a specialist and also has a standard which he must maintain to be worthy of his calling. However, many dog owners are more in need of training than their dogs. The owner should personally do his own dog training if at all possible, for the man who trains a dog will enjoy more success in getting the best performance from him. Even if the dog can already handle game birds, after a fashion, there are always some phases of performance which need improvement and polish, for the average dog can hardly be expected to show much interest in the finer points of accomplishment.

In any event, the dog must know how to do his work, and if the owner is to do the training it follows that he must know more about the proper procedure than the dog. If the owner does not want to learn, the dog must be sent to a trainer, and the owner will still have to learn how to handle the dog while hunting him, otherwise the trainer's work and the money spent on training will be a complete loss.

Most everyone agrees that the best instruction is that learned in the school of experience, but with no helping guide to follow, it is a difficult undertaking to learn the many complexities of dog training. The actual training of a bird dog does not require volumes of words to explain, and an effort has been made to eliminate all non-pertinent information on the following pages. However, it is much easier to learn training procedures by reading a few books on training than it is to start actual training and learn from trial and

error. The written words will give the novice
a training guide to follow. Instead of groping
in the dark he will know what course to
follow in every phase of training and as a
result will be able to do a much better job of
training.

The crux of the matter is that we must
never ask a dog to perform. We must tell him,
and then show him how it is to be done. We
must settle for nothing less than fault-free
performance. To fully enjoy the many thrills
of dog ownership and the hunting of game
birds which go with it, there must be complete understanding and rapport between the
owner and his dog. Or to sum it up in a
simple phrase, with which this book also con-
cludes, "You must learn to handle your dog,
or he will surely handle you."

SHERMAN WEBB
Lebanon, Missouri

I

Selecting
A Bird Dog

The Choice of Breed

Training presupposes something to train, and thus perhaps we should start with a short discussion of the factors that go into selecting a bird dog. Many considerations can enter into your choice, not the least of which is your state of solvency. In general, however, the choice is between setters, pointers and Continental breeds, and the prime considerations are your own personal taste and preference, the species of gamebirds you hunt and the general topography and terrain of the countries you hunt.

For my money, it's hard to make a bad choice — *if* you buy good proven shooting-dog bloodlines. It's rare to find a well-bred dog with insufficient basic talent, whatever the breed. If you look around and ask around in the area in which you plan to hunt, you will quickly learn which breeds generally work out best, on average, but I'm willing to bet that you'll also find some outstanding exceptions. Thus my advice is, pick the breed that appeals to you.

Historically, of course, the English pointer and the English setter have always been the most popular pointing breeds for the upland hunter. I've handled a good many of both, and don't find a lot to choose between them; in fact, I doubt that the discussion of relative merits will ever be conclusively settled.

Perhaps the chief difference between them, aside from coat, is in their relative precocity. I suspect that the man who has owned both pointers and setters over a period of years will generally conclude that on average, pointers come on at an earlier age than setters.

The pointer may give every indication of being a mature dog at the age of one year, while the setter at that stage will often show that he is still a juvenile. The pointer can be expected to do good work the first season he is hunted, but he is more inclined to back-slide and may need a course of training his second season to do as well the second season as he did the first.

In spite of the fact that the setter comes on more slowly, however, I find that, year after year, he tends to be more consistent with his performance. He will often continue to improve until he reaches the zenith of his potential, which may occur only when he reaches the age of four to five.

For many years the various Continental breeds hardly existed in sufficient numbers in the United States to be worth mentioning. In the last decade or so, however, they have started to come into their own, with the Brittany spaniel and the German shorthair making particularly strong upsurges in popularity.

Both the Brit and the shorthair have much to recommend them. The only spaniel that points its game, the Brittany is also versatile enough to make a good wildfowl retriever in areas in which the weather is not too severe. Like the shorthair, it also tends to have a more restricted hunting range and to hunt a bit closer to the gun than the average setter or pointer, which may be an advantage for certain gunners and in certain types of cover. Both breeds are known for their affable character and intelligence, and they want to please, perhaps a bit more than the setter or pointer. This may be due to the fact that they are often less nervous in temperament, and have less innate desire to run. In consequence, many trainers find them somewhat easier to train, and they make ideal dogs for the amateur handler to work with.

The German shorthair does a masterful job of retrieving from water in temperate climates, but his coat is not designed for icy water.

The shorthair pictured on this page retrieves from land or water and is the only two-gaited retriever I ever saw. When retrieving at his normal gallop, if the owner wants to show him off, all he has to do to make him go into slow motion is hold up his hand and say, "Slow." To stop him while retrieving he says, "Whoa." To resume the normal gallop, he says, "Hurry up."

This dog is so biddable he will remain in an open truck at the command "Stay," while other dogs work birds nearby. He had his schooling in the company of a wide-going young pointer, and he learned to run to the limits. As a result, his range is in no way restricted and he will make a good dog hustle to find birds ahead of him. My only justifiable criticism of this dog is his hard-to-see color.

Of the other comparatively new breeds which also make good shooting dogs, the weimaraner and the Hungarian vizsla can be outstanding, and I've heard of good wire-haired pointing griffons and German wire-haired pointers, though I've never worked with any. And then, there are the old traditional Irish setters and Gordon setters, both now pretty much in eclipse as bird dogs, unfortunately. They can still be excellent, if selected from sound shooting-dog strains, but these are hard to find; their popularity as bench and show dogs led many breeders away from gundog bloodlines, and it's hard to breed bird sense back in, once it's been bred out.

On balance, I don't find much to choose between the setter and the pointer. Setter people say the pointer doesn't have enough coat to keep him warm during the winter months, and will not take to heavy cover such as brier thickets and cocklebur-covered terrain; pointer people say the setter has too much hair, cannot stand hot weather well and attracts burrs like a magnet. And so it goes; for every pro there is a con, and the arguments have been going for decades and will probably continue forever. Listen to all the claims and counterclaims, for there is a measure of substance to them, and then pick the breed that suits your own needs and your own personal fancy.

Selecting the Individual

The next question to answer is, "How do you know which individual to pick?" Faced with six or eight apparently healthy puppies, how does the prospective owner decide between them? And at what age should he purchase his dog?

Let's talk first about buying a puppy rather than an older dog. As a general rule, puppies are offered for sale when they reach the age of eight to ten weeks, and the litters get pretty well picked over if you wait much longer. In addition, the younger the puppy is after weaning, the easier it is to gain and hold its confidence and affection. So right after weaning is as good a time as any.

The matter of choosing from among litter-mates is a bit tougher. No man is perfect, and neither is his dog—at least, none that I've ever encountered. But mortal man, with his very limited faculties, has no way of looking at his neighbor from the outside and divining his true worth. And neither can he look at a dog or a puppy, assess its character and confidently say, "This is the best of the lot or the litter." In other words, nobody can invariably select the best puppy, and a considerable amount of luck always enters into the matter of selecting the individual.

As a practical matter, if you purchase the pup from a distant breeder, the selection of the individual becomes his sole responsibility, and sometimes this is as good a way as any — if the kennel is well established and has a good reputation to maintain. In any case, it's better than relying on old wives' tales or strictly eye appeal, which is probably the main factor in the selection of most puppies sold in any given year.

Dog owners give an assortment of reasons for their selection of a certain puppy. Some are common-sense reasons; others are based on hearsay from people who have no information on which to base a conjecture. One so-called knowledgeable buyer may prefer the runt of the litter because he has always been told the runt of the litter invariably turns out to be a real bird dog. Though surely some runts have worked out, this choice, by all sensible standards of reasoning, should be the worst possible one. In these cases, pity may enter into the picture. You must not let yourself be swayed by pity and become saddled with a sorry specimen which may be a headache for his entire lifetime.

Other buyers, seeking to show their uncanny ability to choose the best, most natural bird dog, will look for a puppy with a black palate. Occasionally they may find one and if they do that ends the search, regardless of physical make-up, comparative size, disposition, color, etc. But what effect the roof of a dog's mouth could possibly have on his potential as a shooting dog is far beyond my ken.

When a prospective buyer opens the puppy's mouth I would normally assume that he is inspecting teeth or looking for an undershot or overshot jaw. Sometimes, however, such ideas never enter his head. If you ask him what he is looking for, he may reply with a sheepish grin on his countenance, "I will tell you, but if you laugh . . . " and go on to explain about black palates. Of course this is unadulterated nonsense, based on nothing but superstition.

One might think that a prospective buyer would seek the advice of a qualified person when buying a puppy, rather than be guided by some individual who may never have owned a bird dog and bases his knowledge on ownership of a mixed-breed stock dog. However, many potential buyers have come to me accompanied by just such an "expert."

But even though nobody can select with infallible accuracy, there are some commonsense guidelines to assist you, which will work out a lot of the time. Perhaps the main factors are sound structure, confidence and precociousness.

Each breed has its own standard for conformation or structure, and you should become familiar with the official standard for the breed under consideration. But let's consider the kind of criteria that are involved, using as an example a pointer puppy.

You are looking for a puppy that is fine in

all respects, for even poor puppies are fine in some respects, at least. He should be about 95 percent white, perhaps with liver ears and a blazed face. The more white on his body the easier it will be to see him when hunting him in dense cover or thick woods. It would be preferable to have no large liver, lemon or black spots on his body. His head should be long with a moderately wide skull, the better to hold a lot of brains. His ears should be thin and silky and should lie close to the cheeks. He should have medium-size eyes, soft and dark. His back must be strong, with a firm neck, clean and long. Wide nostrils will aid him in scenting ability. His muzzle should be straight, long and square. He must be deep-chested with a well-sprung ribcage which will permit him to run all day, every day. His feet, a very important feature to consider, should be round, closely set, and well padded with well-arched toes.

This is the conformation all dog owners would like their dog to possess, but only a few will find one with such perfection in conformation.

Even if you get your choice in these respects, you actually have nothing which will give positive assurance he will ever become an acceptable bird dog; but at least you will have a pup of your very own choosing, not another man's spoiled rejection, which is a big step in the right direction.

Of course, many things can happen to this perfect specimen. At any stage of growing up he can develop shyness, although if you have wisely selected a bold puppy there is little likelihood of this happening. He may never develop desire to hunt game birds. He may never develop affection for man. He may become a bolter before his training is completed. He may not have a brain in his beautiful head and may be constantly lost from you while hunting with him, or he may intentionally leave you each time he is taken afield. These are some of the reasons that cause the smart buyer to go only to reputable breeders, who offer young dogs from a strain known for stable character.

Since at best the selection of a puppy from a litter is always a hit-and-miss affair, I repeat that the best way to improve the odds of getting a good one is by starting with a prospect from parents of proven ability. However, while it is impossible to learn much about a two-month-old puppy's mental capacity or scenting ability from brief observation, if the buyer can observe the prospect for a *little* period of time, many points for or against his selection can be sorted out.

Sometimes you can do a lot worse than to pick the puppy that seems to sort of pick you. At any rate, the shy puppy that tends to run whenever a stranger appears, or when something unusual happens, is the one to leave with the breeder.

If you can spend some time watching the litter, you will occasionally notice a puppy who spends a great deal of time looking for something to point—a butterfly, a bee, a fly, anything that moves. I consider this a definite indication of natural tendencies, and a puppy of this type is always a preferred choice. Also, you will be wise to choose one with a look-alive appearance; one who shows interest in everything that goes on in his kennel world, and who looks confidently at you as if to say, "I'm proud of my heritage, and happy to be what I am."

If you want to preserve this kind of attitude, it's often wise, when you buy a puppy, to also purchase one of his brothers or sisters to keep him company. I'm not just being a sentimentalist about this, for in actual fact, it proves beneficial in many ways. One little puppy will miss his brothers and sisters. He will have no playmates and he will be afraid in his dark kennel. Being all alone in his new home he will probably cry all night and interrupt your family's sleep, and even worse, the sleep of your good neighbor. After a few nights of crying you will very likely hear some pointed remarks about your new puppy.

At the time of purchase you must find out from the breeder about vaccination for distemper, leptospirosis, infectious hepatitis, and rabies and worming of the puppy, for if these have not been accomplished, they should be right away. However, any reputable breeder makes a practice of good health care for his dogs and vaccinates and worms all the puppies on a strict schedule.

In assessing the young dog's intelligence

and scenting ability, do not be too hasty. Obviously, we must be reasonably sure he possesses both before large amounts of time and money are spent on his training, though it won't take a competent trainer long to give a correct evaluation of these qualities. But once he's been given a fair chance and proved wanting, we must be ruthless in discarding the time-waster. It's hard enough to make a good dog out of a good prospect, let alone a bad one.

If your chosen specimen loses some of his appeal along the way to becoming a finished shooting dog, by revealing shyness, lack of interest or one of the many other faults a dog can have, you will be money ahead if you part with your sentiment and the dog at the same time and start all over with another puppy. Sentiment and pity have no place in the scheme of things when one is attempting to develop a top shooting dog.

Sources of Purchase

Where is the best place to find the kind of dog you want? On the whole, I believe that the most likely place is a large kennel where hundreds of puppies are whelped each year. No matter how discriminating your demands may be, the big kennel operator is much more likely to have the individual you are looking for, since he always has a much wider range of breed, type, color, disposition and so on to choose from. Moreover, you can usually have more confidence in a large breeder, for the large establishment will depend on having developed and sustained a large clientele of satisfied customers over a period of years. Hence, you are more likely to get full value received at such a place.

Responsible breeders who spend their lifetime in the business as a hobby and/or for profit are always seeking outstanding individuals to improve their kennel blood lines, and are always working to breed out bad qualities and breed in more good qualities. Their young stock will come from sires and dams of proven ability.

Dogs of all breeds and ages are advertised in most sporting magazines and dog magazines by large kennel owners whose integrity is well established, at prices ranging from $50 for a two-month-old puppy to hundreds of dollars for a finished dog. At the other end of the spectrum, however, you can buy all kinds of so-called puppy and older "bird dogs" for as little as $10—without papers, in most cases.

In general, you get what you pay for. The breeding of the $10 wonder is usually untraceable. Most often, the only information you can get on its forebears is that they were bird dogs, though in all too many cases, this is a debatable question, too. For it does not mean that the parents were good, dependable shooting dogs, just that they were bird dogs. And possibly this $10 dog has mixed blood coursing through his veins which doesn't show on the surface. For one reason or another registration papers cannot be furnished, but according to the salesman both sire and dam could have been registered. They may tell you the puppy's parents were top bird dogs, but it might be wise to consider by whose standards the comparisons were made.

When purchasing the $10 dog it should be borne in mind that it will cost as much to feed him, and probably more to train him, than it will a puppy with proven potential. On balance, you will seldom find a true bargain in the $10 or gift dog. If you steer clear of such purported "steals," you will usually come out dollars ahead. Pay the going price to the reputable dealer, a breeder with breed improvement in mind who has built a well-established kennel on the basis of honesty and integrity, and you will rarely have cause for regret.

Buying a Finished Dog

The problems involved when purchasing a puppy or a dog that is not trained should be very carefully considered. If the buyer does not wish to train the dog himself, the cost of professional training must be added to the purchase price. The cost of feed for a puppy two months of age to the age when he becomes old enough to train will run into another $50 which must be counted in the purchase price. Vaccination will run as high as $22 in the larger cities; somewhat less in smaller towns. (However, this cost is generally borne by the reputable breeder.) And last but not least, the dog may turn out to be worthless after time, money and effort have been spent on him. A large percentage of dogs never make the grade.

In other words, the puppy is not always the cheap buy. You should ask yourself these questions: Am I capable of training this young dog? Will he be worth the effort? (This, of course, you will never know until you have tried it.) How will I fare financially in the selection of a puppy over a finished shooting dog?

Finally, you must decide if you have enough time to achieve the standard of training you require by the time the hunting season rolls around. For although it should not take years of training to achieve limited success, substantial success does not come overnight. It does take some time.

Working a dog for twenty minutes each day should have him pointing stanchly and retrieving in one month's time. However, it would be unreasonable to expect that anyone could completely finish a dog in one month, because it cannot be done. The groundwork can be laid, and the owner can, if he chooses and is competent to do it, finish the dog during hunting season. Remember, however, that few hunters like to forego shooting birds when opportunity arises, and instead keep their undivided attention on control of the dog. When hunting during open season no one wants to be constantly correcting a dog.

You may come to the conclusion that buying a finished shooting dog, over the long haul, will create fewer problems and will cost you less, and you may decide your preference will be the finished shooting dog.

What qualifies as a trained dog? It is rare to find two individuals who agree in every detail on the requirements of a finished shooting dog. Everyone has different opinions, both on training and on performance in the field. Many handlers find fault with a dog that circles a covey of running quail and forces them to hold to point, though to me, this is an indication of intelligence and experience. One hunter may prefer his dog to move up as scent becomes faint, indicating that the birds have moved on, and to continue in this fashion until the birds finally hold to point. Yet another may prefer to have his dog hold point until he arrives on the scene, regardless of whether the birds hold or not, and then walk up with him as the dog attempts to pinpoint location of the birds. I prefer the dog that makes decisive points, with the birds in front of him every time he establishes point.

For my money, the mark of the finished shooting dog is when he can be hunted day after day without your ever having to say one word to correct him. Of course, any dog must be told when to look for dead birds, unless he sees the bird fall. The dog with experience, when not steady to wing and shot, will break at shot, run out in front of the hunter, stop and look back at the hunter, awaiting the words which he hopes to hear, "Dead bird, fetch," then scour the coverts looking for the bird. If you miss the bird and say nothing to him, he resumes hunting.

When purchasing a dog which is supposed to be broke—or finished, whichever you may choose to call it—the buyer should demand sufficient trial under field conditions, to determine that the dog does perform in the manner claimed. When the purchase price is a substantial sum of money, the purchaser should get more than one day's trial. If only one day's trial is witnessed, the dog may have an exceptionally good day and the buyer may believe that the seller's claims are justified by the dog's performance. However, the next time out, the dog may not perform so well. On the other hand, the dog may not perform during the first outing but may do a masterful job the second time out. The owner may relate the details of one excellent hunt and make an impressive story, but almost any dog will have a productive day afield once in a while; what we are looking for is a dog that has a productive day every day he is hunted. So in fairness to both parties, and to the dog, more than a one-day trial is necessary.

Buying a trained bird dog is not like buying a non-working dog, for you are buying something in the dog's head—what he knows. For the man who has never seen a bird dog work under hunting conditions, and may not have the slightest concept of what to expect, a trip to the shooting preserve will prove to be an enlightening experience. If the potential buyer will closely observe everything the good dog does in the handling of birds, he will not have to take anyone's word for claims for the purported good dog's performance. He can be witness himself.

Preserve operators cannot afford to use half-finished shooting dogs. They must use the very best money can buy. Preserve dogs are seldom wide hunters because it is not necessary for them to cover ground at a fast, wide pace. The guide knows where the birds were released and can direct the dog to the general area without the client being aware that he is doing so. Hunting close is also preferred on preserves because every bird that is flushed, without the shooter having an opportunity to harvest it, is profit lost—especially so if the birds can fly off beyond the boundaries of the preserve if they are "bumped." A finished shooting dog will save the operator many dollars, whereas the poor dog will lose money through loss of profit from birds not bagged. Repeat customers often request the service of the same dog, visit after visit, if the dog puts on a good performance and they are impressed with his work. The quality of preserve shooting dogs can be the difference between a profitable business and a hard-to-make-ends-meet venture.

Anyone with only one dog for sale may be falsely impressed with the dog and his impression will not be justified by the dog's performance. He will make wild claims for his dog because he is blinded by sentiment. You will pay for part dog, part sentiment, and in many cases you will be buying sentiment only. You must be knowledgeable about bird dogs so that you can answer the question: "What does this man know about dogs?"

Fellowship

The world is a lonely place without friends and fellowship, and this is just as true for your dog as it is for you. Every dog needs social contact every day to stay healthy and balanced, and every dog should have daily association with his owner or trainer. The young dog should also have the company of at least one dog near his age to play with. In fact, any animal—dog, horse, cow, you name it —should have one of his own kind for company. I firmly believe that animals grow to maturity with much more stable character if they have normal opportunities to associate with others of their species.

Man's intimate relationship with dogs goes back very far in history. Many dogs are at their best when living in man's own domicile instead of a kennel, but this is obviously impractical for the professional trainer. However, it should be a hard and fast rule for all owners or trainers to try to develop a close relationship with each dog in their custody, and this should include at least a daily visit to the kennel other than at feeding time for the

A memorable moment (Warwhoops Peter Fargo 765109).

express purpose of socializing with each individual dog. Greet each one with a few affectionate words, letting him know that you enjoy his company. Give each one a pat on the head and scratch him behind the ears. They may not understand all the words, but they will enjoy the treatment. Such a friendly relationship is the very core of a dog's well-being. The more time spent with them, the more affection and understanding will exist between man and his beloved dog. If you are a stranger to your dog, his confidence will be difficult to win and hold.

I suspect that lack of fellowship for the dog contributes to many faults, such as bolting, hunting excessively wide patterns, shyness, lack of stability, and a general I-don't-care-for-you attitude. In fact, I think it contributes to all faults in general.

II

Preliminary Training

Yard Training

The day you bring the puppy home is the day his basic training should start. Nothing very serious, of course, but you can start teaching him to lead almost immediately. Attach a very light lead to his neck and leave it on all the time he is outside of the kennel, so that he will become accustomed to it. As you coax him along, if he resists, simply release the restraint for a time. Don't use force while he is so young. If teaching him to lead becomes a problem, there will be plenty of time to use

force later on, and we will return to this subject later.

Many dog owners consider teaching a dog
to lead relatively unimportant. But it is
impossible to do any worthwhile training
with a dog that is constantly fighting the
check cord.

Little can be expected from a two-month-
old puppy, but he should be taken from the
kennel each day for thirty minutes or so and
allowed to run and play. This is very educa-
tional for him in many ways — it helps to eliminate fear, and will stimulate interest in
everything that goes on in the world outside
his kennel. (It can become a problem to get a
young dog to leave the kennel if he has never
been out of it until the time comes for serious
training. If left in the kennel until he is one
year of age, he will be retarded, and if the dog
is not taken from the kennel and given some
training before he reaches the age of two
years, there is every probability he will never
develop a desire to hunt.)

To start developing the puppy's hunting instincts, every time you take him out for play,
attach a quail wing to a line on a fishing pole
for him (them) to play with. Puppies become
so interested in the quail wing that it may
seem they will never stop chasing it, but
eventually they will tire. After they learn
there is nothing to be gained by chasing
something they cannot catch, they may decide that a sneaky approach is what is called
for, but after many trials they learn it is almost

Teaching the dog to lead is training in its simplest form, but it can be a difficult job with a mature dog. Thus puppies should be taught to lead when very young. At times the dog will completely leave the ground, and at other times one must drag the dog for some distance before he will come on. Don't worry about being too rough; in time even the stubborn case will lead with no difficulties.

impossible to catch something that jumps away just as they get to it, only a few short inches out of their reach.

It is great fun to watch their tactics; to see them sneak up on the quail wing as stealthily as a cat. Here is where one can get an insight into their intelligence. The more intelligent puppy will stop chasing long before the others. For the more persistent ones, throw the wing as far as the length of the line will permit, and then slowly draw the wing toward them. They will stand their ground and wait for the wing to come ever closer until it is within a few inches of their noses, and then they will stiffen into a point. After standing on point for a few minutes they will shift their feet and give every indication they intend to attempt to catch it one more time. They'll get balanced just so, and in they go — only to have it snatched away once more.

All the while this play is going on, you will be using commands that you don't expect them to understand, but which will at least acquaint them with the words. Be sure to pet and praise them each time they point the wing. To start developing their retrieving instinct, use an object such as a soft rubber ball or a corncob which they can chase when you throw it for them. Seldom will a puppy bring the object all the way back to you, but even so, the play will serve as a start in learning to retrieve.

Play training should be a lot of fun for you as well as for the puppy. In fact, I'd say that if you don't find yourself getting a lot of laughs and a lot of enjoyment out of working with puppies, then bird-dog training is probably not for you. One of the great things about training should be the fact that even the work is fun; if it isn't, you probably ought to find something that is.

Rewards and Petting

It shouldn't take any trainer long to realize how important to the puppy praise and petting are. Through praise and petting any dog will become acquainted with the trainer in much less time, and will approve of you more and more with each passing day and with each training session. After a few days of training he will be sitting at the kennel door waiting for you, and his joy will know no bounds when you open the kennel door and say. "Come on."

Many trainers give small bits of food to reward satisfactory performance. There is merit in this manner of achieving training results, if the dog is of the cooperative temperament and is intelligent, but not all dogs are endowed with their fair share of intelligence, and for those that are not, it will take more than praise and petting to accomplish the desired results. However, that still doesn't mean that praise and petting should be omitted when dealing with a dog of this temperament. If you work or hunt with more than one dog, be sure that you don't

After a dog has done a good job of retrieving, show him by words and deed that you are pleased with his performance. Pet him, rub him behind the ears, tell him that he is a good dog. It will make him want to do everything in the proper manner, and he will love you all the more.

bestow all your praise and petting on your favorite dog. It is not fair to ignore any dog, even one you think deserves little consideration.

It usually takes more than the hope of petting to correct problems in the mature dog, for the wrongdoing rewards him itself unless something less pleasant comes along with it. However, that can all come later. There's little need for stern correction in working with the young puppy, and it's hard to overdo the reward of praise and petting. Now is the time for him to build up his confidence in and affection for you, so don't hesitate to make a fuss over him for relatively modest achievements.

Teaching the Puppy to Come and to Stop

Each time the puppy is taken out of the kennel, open the gate and say "Come." At first he will be reluctant to leave the kennel, but after a few times he will be sitting at the gate waiting for you. He will learn to remain in the kennel until you say "Come."

Since "Whoa" is the most important command a dog must learn, it is important that it be started early in the dog's training. But since it is impossible to enforce the command when one has no means of restraining the puppy, final training of this command should wait until the puppy is six months of age. In the meantime, when you can lay your hands on the puppy, perhaps as he runs by, hold him and give him the command "Whoa." Lift his tail in a pleasing position, place your hand under his chin, and pet him. In time he will learn to pose in this position like a model. It is always a delight to show your friends how biddable the puppy is; how pretty he is in his pose. Even more delightful is the fact that later in the puppy's life, whenever you say "Whoa," he will assume this breathtaking pose.

If your three-month-old puppy, perhaps one month in training, will only come when called and more or less whoa, don't be impatient with his progress. You still have plenty of time before he is to become a finished product.

Teaching the Puppy to Sit and Lie Down

Teaching a dog to sit is one of the easier lessons to teach, and on many occasions it is handy to have a dog that will sit on command. I usually teach it as soon as the puppy understands what "Whoa" means and will whoa upon command without hesitation. I tell him to whoa, and when he stops, I walk up to his side, grasp him by the muzzle and lift his head, at the same time placing one hand on his hindquarters and gently forcing him down. You may have to restrain him in this position for a while, at first, but after a lesson or two, he will remain in the "sit" position until told to "come on." Pet him each time he does it. Repeat the lesson until he will sit upon command.

Once the dog has learned to sit, it is easy to teach him to lie down on command. Put him in the sit position, and tell him, "Down." To enforce the command, take his front feet in one hand and draw them out in front of him, at the same time exerting pressure on his shoulders. He can go nowhere except down. Hold him in this position, repeating the command "Down" and petting him all the while

To teach the dog to sit, place your right hand around his muzzle and lift his head, at the same time pressing down on his hindquarters with the left hand.

he is there. He is less likely to attempt to get up if you pet him, but if he does attempt to rise, say "No," and restrain him. Continue repetition of the lesson until he will down on command and will remain in that position until released by the words "Come on." To test him, walk away from him a distance of twenty-five yards and let him remain in the down position for twenty minutes or so.

If you allow him to leave the down position before you release him with the command "Come on," it is a breach of discipline, and once he gets away with it he will try again and again.

Each time you take the dog from the

To teach the dog to lie down, have him sit, then straighten his front legs out and press down on his shoulders. Force him to stay in this position for progressively longer periods. To test him, walk away twenty-five yards or so. Eventually he will remain down indefinitely if you don't release him.

kennel, be sure to run through the "Whoa," "Sit," "Down," and other commands he learns as his training progresses. Maintain obedience to all commands by requiring correct execution of each phase of training before you continue on to the next phase of training. Methodical consistency is what produces results.

The Trainer's Voice

From the very earliest training sessions, always remember that if the dog is to end up under complete control, the trainer must start with complete control of his emotions, his actions, and his voice. Accordingly, in teaching voice commands, never raise your voice above normal level. After all, the dog's hearing is five times better than yours, so there is no need for shouting. A softly spoken word will still be heard and the response will often be better than if a loud, boisterous tone of voice is used. If you speak to a dog in a shrill or strident tone of voice, it will only serve to make him nervous and to distract him from his work. It will also tell him you are unsure of what you are trying to accomplish. It is very important that he have confidence in your ability if you are to get the best performance from him.

On the other hand, a teacher who speaks with faltering words hesitatingly, without confidence, can scarcely hope to inspire confidence in his pupil, the dog in this instance. It is most difficult to get through to a dog if you yourself seem timid and unsure of yourself. So be definite, but not shrill, right from the beginning. When you see some guy yelling his head off at his dog, and getting nowhere, you'll be glad you did.

Perfecting the Fundamentals

The puppy, now perhaps four months of age, will come, whoa, sit, and lie down. If there are any special niceties of training you want your dog to know, or tricks such as sitting up, they should prove an easy task once you have come this far. By now you should appreciate that the training of a dog takes a lot of time and patience, but also realize that training is fun and that the sense of achievement is most gratifying.

From here on, through all of his training, it is advisable to gradually be more insistent that the young dog perform to perfection. Continue to go through his routine each day, but invent new tests for him. For example, to test him on 'Whoa," put him on whoa and hide behind a building or tree. See how long he will stand. If he leaves the whoa position, go to him, rap him gently, pose him, all the while saying "Whoa," and test him again. Of course, don't let him stand until he is completely bored—five minutes is enough for now. Later on, however, you can make him stand for thirty minutes.

The puppy's education is coming along nicely, but it is only the beginning. There is much to do until he becomes a finished dog. Up to now, the training has been pretty much play, and little or no physical force has been involved. From the age of six months on, however, training becomes more serious.

Introducing the Check Cord

There are many more dogs of all ages that will not lead properly than dogs that will.

Few hunting dogs will walk obediently at heel, with or without a leash—they tug at the leash, go this way, that way, run around the handler, get choked from pulling on the leash and drag the handler hither and yon. This must not be tolerated. If the dog is uncontrollable when the means of control are attached to his collar, how can you expect to control him when all means of control are removed?

By the time the puppy is five or six months old, he is old enough to start some serious field training, so it is high time to teach him how to lead correctly. Teaching the puppy to lead involves familiarizing him with the check cord for the first time. Some trainers introduce it much earlier, but I feel that it is illogical to use a check cord on a two-month-old puppy. There is seldom any need for restraint on such a young dog. However, when he reaches the age when he starts to have ideas of his own, such as going where he pleases, ignoring commands, etc., then it is time to acquaint him with the check cord.

Teaching a dog to lead is a minor detail—training in its simplest form—yet it's very important that this first stage of training is accomplished properly. With big, strong dogs it may take some muscle to get the job done right. An easy way to prepare to teach a dog to lead is to tie him with a chain in a place where he can do no harm to himself, and leave him there until he learns to get around without becoming entangled in the

Start the young dog off with the check cord attached to his collar and with the rope half-hitched around the stake.

When he points pose him as you like to see him.

Lift his tail high, pet him. Tell him he is the best dog you ever saw and make him believe it. It is important that he does believe it.

When he performs perfectly, remove the check cord and let him seek and find the bird. When he does, tell him again how he pleases you. Pet him. He'll love it.

chain. However, make certain that he cannot climb over some object and become suspended, for he can easily choke to death.

The check cord has a snap on one end and a loop in the other end. Twenty feet of quarter-inch nylon rope is long enough and strong enough for the dog up to six months of age. For large, powerful dogs the check cord should be made of half-inch rope.

The loop on one end of the check cord comes in handy when both hands are needed while working the dog. The loop saves the loss of skin and prevents rope burns. A large dog with a lot of go power can be difficult to keep under control even with a check cord.

The check cord is attached to the collar, of course. Many trainers customarily use it with a chain "choke collar," or in difficult cases, with a force collar which works on the choke-collar principle but has spikes on the inside.

I do not believe that a force collar should ever be used on a young dog unless there is no other way to get obedience from him. However, it is a bother to use an ordinary collar on the young dog in training. I often use a leather collar made like a choke collar but without spikes. It is easy to slip this collar over the dog's head and it is easily removed when finished with the dog after daily training.

After the dog reaches the age of six months and is still quite headstrong, the force collar can be used if necessary. The dog that pulls and tugs on the spike collar soon learns to leave some slack in the check cord when he feels the sharp spokes on his tender skin. As in all phases of training, of course, the characteristics of each dog must be considered. The timid dog may yelp each time he feels the collar tighten even if he feels no pain, while the bold dog may show no indication of discomfort even when the spikes dig into his skin. So use some common sense.

Admittedly, a large older dog that has never been on a check cord will try your patience. If he decides to run back to the more familiar surroundings of the kennel and catches you off guard, he may almost pull your arm out of its socket. However, loud words will neither ease your pain nor help him. Speaking in low tones while the pain is still running through your arm may seem difficult, but do it. Don't let your own carelessness cause you to punish the dog. He doesn't know any better; you do. If you permit yourself to become loud and angry, the dog may become afraid of you and your training problems will be even more difficult.

Before the dog discovers that he can go only so far, he may run circles around you and wrap the check cord around your legs (or leg, if he goes between your legs). If you are slow to react you may get spilled on the ground and perhaps lose some skin from your shin bones, for a puppy can wrap coils of the check cord around you faster than you can remove them.

When a puppy runs behind you, he will seldom return by the same route, but will go all the way around, forcing you to change hands with the check cord. This can become annoying, especially if you have something in the other hand. Dealing with this will give the aspiring trainer plenty of chances to exercise his self-control, for you will learn that it is normal behavior for many dogs.

If the dog has a friendly disposition—and most bird dogs do—he will want to jump up on you at every opportunity, sometimes raking your legs with his claws, perhaps even removing a bit of skin. Some trainers recommend stepping on the dog's hind feet, but there is a much better cure: As you lift your knee in self-defense, inadvertently (let the dog think it accidental) let the knee make solid contact with his chest. Your knee may tip him over and if he has the normal amount of intelligence, he will decide to stand on his own four feet and not on your two feet.

How do you get a dog to come along with you if he simply lies down and refuses to budge? You just drag him along until he's had enough. Some of the more obdurate dogs will lie on the ground and permit themselves to be dragged for as far as fifty feet, mouth hanging open, scooping up grass, leaves and dirt, before they get on their feet to get a lungful of air; then they'll lie down again for more dragging.

With such a defiant dog, one that sulks like an opossum, you will get poor response until he realizes he is fighting a losing cause, and has nothing to fear.

After a few trips to the training area many a dog will become so interested in his work that in his desire to get where the birds are to be found, he will drag you, if permitted to do so. Of course he must be restrained, but this is a good problem to be faced with. On the whole, however, leading isn't a difficult thing for a trainer to teach or improve — it just needs to be done, and the earlier it's accomplished, the easier it makes everything else.

Obedience

Teaching a dog obedience is really the main purpose of training. If one can control a dog, all problems are easier to cope with. In practice, obedience can best be taught along with more specific lessons; yard training for the sole purpose of teaching commands is not as essential as some trainers think. You can teach a dog to whoa while he stands on point on game birds just as well as, and perhaps better than, when he is just standing.

The first thing to remember is that the trainer must always be in a position to enforce obedience each time a command is given. If you are not in a position to enforce a command, do not give it. If you are unable to force the dog to do your bidding when you command him the first time, there is no point in repeating the command, only to have it ignored the second time.

Contrarily, when he learns that he has no alternative but to obey commands, you have

"Whoa!" This German shorthair pointer stops on command midway through a retrieve.

made considerable progress. When he will whoa on command without the slightest hesitation, he may still be far from a finished dog, but he will cause little trouble when you are hunting him with finished dogs, and you can wait for him to come more slowly. As he gains experience he will learn to honor on sight without command.

The second important principle is that you must never allow a dog to commit a mistake without making on-the-spot correction. If you wait for some time to do the correcting, he will have forgotten what he did wrong and the correction will mean nothing to him. And if the dog does not know what he did wrong, the correction will serve no purpose.

Of course, correction can and must take many forms. Most often a word or two will serve as sufficient on-the-spot correction to let the dog know that he did something wrong. (With a hard-headed older dog, however, this will not suffice, and then some stronger deterrent force must be brought to bear. You have a problem, and dog-training problems don't go away simply because you ignore them, any more than others do. Hence it is better to attempt to solve the problem while it is still a little problem.)

Needless to say, it is important that the punishment should always fit the crime. Common sense suggests that the first offense should receive first-offense punishment. The trainer must always be positive the dog knows he is guilty of misbehavior and administer light punishment to see if it will deter repeated misbehavior, but if it fails, what course is left open except more severe punishment? Regardless of the novice trainer's opinion, I have a feeling that before he is finished training his first dog, he will agree in principle that this method is the only sensible solution to his many problems.

Punishment is never cruelty when applied in a common-sense manner. It is never necessary to do physical harm to the dog to get positive results. The trainer who flies into rage when training or punishing a dog will never be able to do an effective job. He must con-tain his emotions at all times, and after working with dogs for a while he will come to accept this statement as fact.

Ear pulling is the principal means of punishment resorted to by many owners, and it is most foolhardy. If the dog's ear is pulled and twisted there is a good chance of causing a hematoma in the ear, which may give the dog lasting pain and a very unsightly ear.

In a fit of temper some owners kick their dog or strike him on his sensitive nose. This is cruel treatment and should never be resorted to. You should punish the dog in the same manner as you would a child whom you love.

Many dog owners will admit that they have no knowledge of training procedures, yet state that they are opposed to punishment and object to the professional trainer's methods. How can so many dog owners be so naive?

If you do not consider it important for you to be in charge when training and hunting your dog, the instruction contained in this book will be of little value to you. If you disagree with portions of training procedure outlined herein, do not follow that portion of instruction. If you are of the opinion that you can do a good job of training without resorting to punishment, for example, by all means do not punish your dog. If you can successfully train a dog without resorting to punishment at times, you have no need for instruction, because you are already a better trainer than anyone I am acquainted with.

Field Experiences for the Young Dog

As soon as you can lead and handle the puppy pretty well, he should be taken for short trips afield at every opportunity. These trips will teach him many things which he must learn sooner or later, and if you want to avoid much frustration when hunting him during open season, this is the time to let him learn how to get through or over fences and across deep ditches or bodies of water, and to become acquainted with farm animals. It will also help him to get over the awkward stage much quicker. With these experiences behind him he can then concentrate on hunting and will spend less time exploring every strange object he comes across. Dogs that have never been afield are afraid of large rocks and stumps, and animals of all kinds. They should have the opportunity to learn not to be afraid of these objects before being hunted.

In addition, the young, inexperienced dog will waste a lot of time exploring every scent he comes in contact with, and there are hundreds of such scents to attract his attention. Seemingly it takes forever for the young dog to recognize the sound of a quail flushing and to associate the sound with the bird. It is quite a letdown for the handler to see his young dog come upon a quail and flush it without scenting it, but then give no indication that anything unusual has happened, or that his interest has been the least bit aroused. However, no trip afield is completely without benefit.

Once the puppy reaches the point where he shows interest when he smells bird scent, and starts to surge out and seek this scent, flash-point birds and chase rabbits, then the field trips become more interesting and profitable for the dog, and the handler can see some accomplishment in the training mission.

Though bad habits, such as chasing rabbits and birds, must not be allowed to become too deeply ingrained at this time since they will have to be corrected later on, with some dogs there is no other way to stimulate interest. If desire is dormant the only way to stimulate it is to let him, or even encourage him, to chase any animal that runs (except farm animals) and every bird that flies. A possible exception is mice, for if positive action is not taken to discourage puppies from pointing mice at a fairly early age, it can grow to become quite a problem. If the dog is permitted to pursue his search for mice, he may become more interested in them than in game birds. (At the risk of starting a controversy, I will state that young pointers are more often guilty of pointing mice than setters.)

While the dog is still young, a little gruff talk, just to let him know you are not interested, is generally sufficient to make him stop it, but I have known owners who did nothing to dissuade their dog and the dog became a confirmed mouse pointer. To ignore it leads the dog to believe you approve of it. I have seen top prospects develop into habitual mousers.

It is frustrating, to say the least, to see a young dog make a beautiful point and to walk up behind him, ready for the flush of a covey of birds, only to have him jump in and start making the dirt fly. Don't let your dog get the habit.

If you are lucky enough to have some kill-deer (plover) in your area, you will find that they make one of the best possible quarries to stimulate the "birdy" instincts of the young dog, even in cases in which other induce-ments have failed. The killdeer is a shorebird which is found near ponds where ground cover is sparse. His flight is short, circular and erratic. He remains on the ground most of the time, and when flushed by the young dog, remains airborne only long enough to put

This young English setter displays pleasing style when pointing game birds, but there is much to be desired when pointing pigeons. This is understandable, because a pigeon is not a game bird.

some distance between him and the chasing dog, then will settle down on the ground where the dog can have another go at him.

The killdeer's plaintive cry is a further inducement to the dog's interest. His legs are long for his body size, being almost out of proportion, but they serve their purpose for wading the shallows in search of food. He is a fast runner and when molested may disappear only to reappear perhaps twenty-five yards distant from the spot at which he was last seen by the dog. This will make the young dog use his nose to locate the bird. He will be in a frenzy in his eagerness to find the hiding bird and do some more chasing.

This makes an ideal situation to stimulate the pup's latent desire. Such a milieu will make most any young dog get off your heels and keep him off. You will have trouble catching the dog when the day's fun is over, because he will be most unwilling to leave such a fun place.

It may seem to you that this would be an ideal time to introduce the dog to gunfire were not the shooting of killdeer strictly illegal. It is true that after the dog has been permitted to chase plover for an hour or so on several occasions it is very doubtful that even a dog with the most retiring disposition would pay the slightest attention to the report of gunfire. However, it costs nothing to avoid any possible chance of making the dog gunshy. He has not yet started serious training and you will have countless ideal situations to fire the critical, initial round later on. However, when you do fire the first shot over him, you must make certain that the dog is in hot pursuit of a bird of some species.

III

Serious Training

Training Requirements

All trainers prefer to work with a dog that has had no previous training, unless the dog is too old to have any interest in game birds. The dog with no previous training is unlikely to have serious man-made faults to deal with, and it is usually much easier to keep a dog from developing faults than it is to correct defects that have already become established. Thus I am going to assume in this section on finishing the bird dog that you are working with a puppy that you have brought along

56

Log and brush piles hinder training.

yourself, and have no established faults to cope with. (In the next part we will go into the problems of the older dog and how to cope with them.)

To finish the bird dog's training you need three things: you need a dog, a place to work the dog, and birds to work him on.

You may not have a lot of choice regarding your training field, for an ideal bird field may not be readily available to you. However, almost any field that has a little cover will do in a pinch. I would never argue that the pointer is an ideal companion in a city apartment, but still, the pleasures of bird-dog training need not be restricted to the dog owner living in rural areas. The determined, dedicated owner who must live in the city or suburb can train a dog in his own back yard if he uses enough imagination and perseverance. A bird dog can be taught to whoa in the confines of a basement or living room, if needs be. He can be taught to sit, to lie down and to come when called. He can be taught force retrieving; in fact, an isolated place such as a basement is ideal for this particular kind of training. The appendix includes a brief description of this technique. He can be worked on birds with the use of a pigeon, which can be kept in an orange crate or similar small enclosure.

I am not saying that this is the ideal way, but it is possible. Of course, a dog trained under these conditions will be unfamiliar with field conditions at first, but most will quickly learn how and where to hunt for game birds when finally taken to the open spaces during the hunting season.

Using Live Birds in Training

The third requirement for advanced bird-dog training—live birds—is the easiest of the three to fulfill. In the old days, trainers sought locations where an extensive supply of wild game was available, but more recently, the use of the lowly pigeon and pen-raised game birds have revolutionized the whole art of training bird dogs. I like to use both, for slightly different purposes, and I firmly believe that anyone can achieve more results with pigeons and pen-raised quail in two weeks than he could hope to accomplish in two months with wild birds.

For the early work on live birds, I prefer to use pigeons. They have a number of outstanding advantages, the first one being that they can be used during any season of the year. In seasons in which it would be virtually impossible to do any training on wild quail because of hot weather and the nesting season, a dog can still work pigeons very well.

In addition, pigeons are easy to work with; they are simpler to catch when penned than game birds, and much cheaper to purchase. One can often pick up as many as one hundred from an abandoned barn, and neighbors who know that you use them for training will often call and ask you to take them for nothing. They want to rid themselves of what they consider a nuisance.

I like to switch over to pen-raised quail for later stages of training, but most dogs can be trained to point stanchly, to honor and to retrieve with the exclusive use of pigeons. I might mention that hatchery quail cost from $1.25 to $2.50 a bird, and the trainer cannot afford to shoot many birds over a dog in training unless the owner is willing to pay the additional cost of the quail. So there are a lot of reasons for using pigeons at first, and no disadvantages that I can think of.

Before the first training session, prepare your training field by driving a strong wooden or iron stake into the ground, somewhere where there is some appropriate cover for planting birds. The stake should be driven into the ground for eighteen inches or two feet, leaving another two or three feet above ground level. The purpose of the stake is to give you a means of restraining the dog when he decides to forget about you and jump in and flush the bird. Whenever you want the dog to be stanch, you need only take a half-turn of the check cord around the stake; you can then move ahead of the dog to move or flush the bird while still maintaining complete control over the dog.

If you are going to be training more than one dog, you should also set up a chain from which leads can be dropped, to which you can snap your other pupils while they are waiting their turn. Obviously, this chain

A double half-hitch around the stake will hold the dog while you attend to planting pigeon.

Young dogs on the chain, eagerly awaiting their turn to perform on pigeons.

should not be right on top of the bird area, but it is important that it should have a good view of it. Nothing helps to arouse a dog's interest in the proceedings like watching his kennel mate having all the fun.

You should have a small canvas bag with a zipper on it to carry the pigeons in. If working more than one dog, you can carry a sufficient number of birds to work a number of dogs and it will save time and trips to the pigeon pen. The bag will hide the birds from the dog, which will give the training a more natural setting. Hang the pigeon bag on a low branch of a nearby tree where it will be handy and out of reach of the dog.

First Training Sessions

At last the preliminaries are over and we are ready to start the serious business of transforming a raw prospect into a finished bird dog.

It is of utmost importance for the dog to be under control at all times during training, so put the check cord on him. He will obediently come to the training area because you have already trained him to lead. (Tomorrow, if he is the brainy type, you will see a great change in him. He will be so anxious to get to the training area you will have difficulty in restraining him in his eagerness.)

While walking the dog to and from the training area, occasionally jerk him up short with the check cord and command him with "Whoa." The word "whoa" is by far the most important word in the dog's vocabulary. When he hears it he has no alternative but to stop if he is restrained by the check cord. Walk up to him, stoop down to his level, pose him in a picturesque stance and pet him. Say to him, over and over, "Good boy," and say his name.

When you give the command "Whoa," have it understood beyond a doubt he must stop without restraint being put on him. He must learn to obey the command unhesitatingly, and when he will do it every time his training has come a long way.

The dog in training will soon learn the check cord is one of the tools of training and will hold still while you slip the collar over his head. Now he is ready.

When you jerk him up short with the check cord and say "Whoa," let him stand a few minutes, all the while making a big fuss over him, then tap him lightly on the head and say, "Come on." He won't see the sense in stopping so many times, since he is in a big hurry, so don't do it too often at the start of the training sessions.

When you get to the training area, snap your dog to a drop chain (or tie him to a tree), and prepare a pigeon for him to work with. Take a pigeon from the bag and pull the flight feathers from its left wing. (The flight feathers are the first eight feathers nearest the wing tip.) Do not pull more than eight; the remaining feathers will help the bird to move faster along the ground, and the faster it goes, the harder it will be for the dog to catch it. The longer it takes the dog to catch the bird the more excited he will become, and excitement will create interest, which is the crux of training at this point. All training efforts will become stagnant without interest.

It is not necessary to make the pigeon dizzy for the first few lessons, because it will take just a few minutes to accomplish what you need do. You want the dog to be aware of the pigeon's presence by scenting it, and if he does not scent it he must see it in order to know it is there. Some dogs will ignore the scent until they have worked the pigeon a few times and become acquainted with the scent. Simply place the pigeon's head under its right wing and lay it on the ground, right wing down. With all the right wing feathers intact, they will shut out the light and it will remain in this position. Stick the pigeon under dead grass or cover it with a few dead leaves, just enough to break up its outline. This will camouflage it so the dog will not see it and sight-point, perhaps aided by slight scent. Sight-pointing is all right for the first few lessons, but if the dog is able to see the bird, he is more likely to jump in and flush the bird if he catches you with a slack check cord. If he points by scent rather than by sight he is less likely to know the exact spot where the bird is, and will be less anxious to jump in on the bird.

Straighten the pigeon's feet out and with its head under its wing it will not work its feet or get them entangled in grass. (This might enable it to get to its feet and perhaps walk away before you are ready with the dog.) Make all your movements deliberate, and be firm in handling the dog, and this will impress upon the dog's mind that you know your business of training. When an owner first starts training dogs, in his anxiety and excitement, he may have a quaver in his voice which the dog will recognize as inexperience, and he will take advantage of the trainer.

Untie the dog and lead him upwind to a point near the pigeon and find out if he can

Disturb the bird with your foot, making it rise on its feet.

smell the bird. Using the check cord wrapped around the stake, move ahead of the bird and allow the dog to move closer if he gives no indication that he smells the bird. Disturb the bird with your foot, which will cause it to take its head from under its wing and stand on its feet. It will generally remain in this position until it gains its bearings. The dog is almost certain to detect the pigeon's movement, but if he doesn't, hold the dog's head within inches of the pigeon. When you push his head down he will resist at first and it sometimes takes a little muscle; however, you will know when he scents or sees the bird, be-

The dog tries to flush the bird with his feet.

The dog soon learns he cannot jump in on the bird.

cause he will quit resisting and immediately relax in the pointing position.

Disturb the pigeon again with your foot and it will walk away or make a fluttering attempt to fly. When the dog sees it apparently making good its escape, chances are he will be after the pigeon like a cat after a mouse. He may show fear of the pigeon for a time, but sooner or later, he will immediately grab the pigeon at every opportunity.

When he attempts to jump in on the pigeon he will fail because you have him under control with the check cord looped around the restraining stake.

When the dog points, stoop down to his level and stroke him along the back, all the while telling him in low tones that he is a good dog and calling him by name. Repeat the words over and over. Handle him; pose him in a pleasing style. Show him by word and action that he has pleased you; that he is doing it just right. Should he point the pigeon and retrieve it at the first trial, you will not have to feign sincerity with your praise. But whether you are sincere or not, you must get the message across to him that you believe he is the greatest. It will pay undreamed-of dividends.

When the dog points, praise him and adjust his position.

Hold his tail in the position of the hands of a clock at high noon while he is on point. Run your fingers up and down on the underside of his tail. He will love all the attention you are giving him. Perhaps he has never known such affectionate treatment and he will absorb it as a sponge absorbs water.

Should he assume a crouching stance on point, or if he is not standing as high as you like, place your hand under his stomach and raise him to stand in a position more to your liking. When he is posed to your satisfaction, lift his hindquarters off the ground a few inches by taking hold of his tail close to his body, then gently lower him to the ground. He may not approve of being lifted by his tail (some do; some don't), but he will grow accustomed to it very quickly and won't mind in the least. This seems to have a tendency to make most dogs more stanch on point.

Some books on training state that upsetting a dog with the check cord will cause him to be steady on point. I could never get enough muscle behind the upset to give the dog any lasting memory of the incident. However, there is another way to give him something to remember indefinitely: Put the check cord on the dog in the usual manner, but then run a half-hitch around the body with the hitch around his flanks. When he hits the end of the rope, the hitch of course tightens. Just what he thinks of it I do not know, but one thing I do know, he sure will hesitate to have it happen to him again.

Dogs with a lot of strength and an obdurate disposition never seem to pay much attention to the check cord, even with the spike collar. A half-hitch around his flanks will cause him to take notice.

While hunting him, if he has a lapse of memory on occasion, cut a section from a fairly large truck tire innertube about two inches in width and put this around his body at the flank and let him wear it for a while. You will be amazed at the difference in his handling. Don't allow the section of innertube to fit too snugly around his flanks, which might interfere with breathing or other body functions—just snugly enough to make him aware that it is there. At times you may be compelled to put the check cord back on him for a few man-sized jerks. His brain capacity will determine how often this must be done.

When you have handled him, petted him and told him repeatedly, "Good boy, Jack," or whatever his name may be, place your hand on his rear end and give a gentle push. He will resist with all his strength, and he will not allow you to push him in on the bird. It is strange, because even though he intends to jump in and attempt to flush the bird, he wants to do it on his own, and doesn't want assistance from you. Of course, the dog should never be allowed to reach the pigeon without your permission.

If he doesn't point the pigeon, however frustrating it may become, there is nothing

You will seldom find a dog that will allow himself to be pushed in on birds. If you lift him by the tail, be careful, especially with a dog weighing fifty or sixty pounds. Grasp the tail close to the body.

you or anyone can do to make him point until he is ready. You can only continue with the training, day after day, in the hope that one day he will point. A few dogs never do point a bird, but generally they are dogs that are too old to become interested. (Last fall I worked a dog that never developed desire, because of deferred training. She was two years of age and had never been worked. The only time she showed the slightest interest was when the pigeon walked away and hid. She watched it until it was hidden, then she leisurely walked over and brought it back. If the pigeon did not hide, she ignored it.)

When the dog has pointed the pigeon and has stood point for five minutes or so (later you can let him stand longer), while you have gone on praising him and handling him, occasionally attempting to push him in on the bird, it is time to disturb the pigeon again. Make the pigeon walk or attempt to fly away and this will create great excitement in the dog.

He may attempt to catch the bird very quickly or he may run past the pigeon yet make no attempt to pick it up, and do so countless times before he ever decides to pick one up. This will create frustration about as quickly as anything you will encounter while training dogs. What can you do? You can hardly force a dog to pick up a running, dodging pigeon, yet you must praise him and act as if you are satisfied with the performance. In fact, you are stalemated. Progress stops but the training effort must continue unless you are willing to concede defeat. If you are persistent, one day your work will be rewarded, but at times it is slow progress.

Throw the pigeon out five or six feet and try to induce him to fetch it. He will be more prone to fetch short casts than long ones at the start. When he grows accustomed to retrieving you can throw it any distance and he will retrieve it time after time.

Make it a steadfast rule to stop training for the day after he has completed a retrieve in good form, or has done a good job on any phase of his training, for that matter. This will keep his interest at a high level because he will remember the good work as the last thing he did.

Many trainers make a practice of giving the bird's head to the dog as further inducement to retrieve, but I don't believe in it. You will defeat your whole purpose if the dog gets the idea that all birds are killed for his benefit, and takes to eating birds on his own. How can you punish a dog today for chewing and eating birds today, and then give him part of a bird tomorrow? The practice of feeding bird heads to the non-retriever might be a great inducement for him to find birds, but for the retrieving, shooting dog it is a poor policy.

When you throw the bird out for him and he doesn't run after it, you must run after it as if it is your intention to beat him to it. This competition will often make a dog more anxious to get to the bird. But don't run fast!

Make it appear that you can't catch the bird (and many times you can't), and he may decide to help you. If he doesn't show interest in this maneuver, hold the pigeon by one wing and let it flutter in his face, while you jog along with the dog at your side. Use any means that come to mind to awaken his interest and to see it does not wane; his interest needs constant stimulation. Once you can get him to hold the bird in his mouth, there is smoother sailing ahead. The use of live pigeons to teach a dog to retrieve is far better than the use of a dummy of any type.

There will be times when certain dogs may misunderstand your command of "Fetch," and may think you are telling them to drop it. If the dog does drop the bird, go out and pick it up, and when you again throw it, don't say anything and he will fetch it all the way. When he comes all the way, stoop to his level to receive the bird, and to pet him. He will come to you more readily when you are in the kneeling position, perhaps because he likes to think he is your compeer.

He has just accomplished a new phase of training and you must show him, by praise, that he has done an excellent job. When you see his reaction to the praise and petting you will realize that it makes a large contribution to success in training. The results will show more clearly at the next training session when he goes out, unconcerned, and retrieves the pigeon as if he were a veteran. When he associates the command "Fetch" with the action, you should have no further problems.

As a general rule retrieving can be taught in one or two lessons. Once a dog retrieves a bird, there is no need to hurry further retrieving lessons because he will get opportunities for improvement each time he is worked.

Some dogs are very delicate retrievers, probably fearful of hurting the pigeon. They may get hold of just a wing, his head, or the lower body section of the bird and drag it to you. Or they may drag the pigeon a short way, drop it, playfully jump back, catch it again and come on with it. This is retrieving the trainer likes to see as a start, because it is almost certain the dog will never develop hard mouth. Trainers are always concerned about hard-mouth retrieving, and it is a real cause for concern.

When the dog shows great desire to retrieve, make him use his nose to locate the pigeon. This is accomplished by throwing the bird in high weeds or dense cover where it can hide. This will make the dog scour the covert in an attempt to locate the bird.

If a dog works his jaws while retrieving a bird to you, it is evident he is chewing it and it will be breathing its last breath. This is a serious problem and must be corrected as soon as possible. After you have taken the bird from him, as carefully as possible, place the dog's upper lips over his upper teeth and exert pressure with your hands. If the dog is intelligent, this may eliminate the trouble, but generally it doesn't come that easy.

When the dog retrieves to hand but is reluctant to release the bird, don't attempt to take the bird away by force. If you do you may cause the dog to become hard-mouthed.

If he retrieves the bird gently but is reluctant to give it to you, be very careful in the manner in which you go about getting him to release it. When you get hold of the pigeon's wing, leg, or other part of the bird's body, if the dog pulls, immediately release your hold. If you pull and he pulls, it is certain to make him resist releasing it and will further contribute to his being hard-mouthed. Many dogs are made hard-mouthed in this thoughtless manner.

Never be in a hurry to take the pigeon from him unless it is evident he is chewing it, but then, of course, get it away from him as soon as possible. Otherwise, let him carry it around for a time. He will enjoy it and this will create more interest and make him want to retrieve every bird he finds or sees fall to the gun. Retrieving is a more or less natural trait in every breed of bird dog.

Do not let the dog retrieve more than two or three times the first lesson. It will be evident when he starts to have less enthusiasm. When he shows the slightest reluctance, stop and let him have time to digest the lesson. Some dogs will lose interest more quickly when working pigeons than when working game birds.

Put the dog in the kennel and you will be amazed at his willingness to leave the kennel the following day, though yesterday you may have had to run him down in the kennel to catch him.

Even though the dog is not doing any strenuous work while in training I believe it is a good policy to give him a day off occasionally. I believe it will give him more incentive to want to get back to training. It will give him time to ponder what he has learned and will help to build his interest in his work. He will show you he has been thinking about his lessons when he rushes to the training area as fast as you and the check cord will permit, and scours the area for a bird to point. When he goes to the exact spot where he found the bird before you will realize he has a memory. (When he does this, it is also time to change the planting spot.)

Once more I will mention the importance of praise; pour it on when he does the job to your satisfaction. Don't ever get the mistaken idea that "praise" talk is a waste of words. He will understand more words than you ever thought him capable of, especially when action gives meaning to the words.

Training with Pen-Raised Quail

If you are so inclined you can continue working with the pigeon until the dog is letter-perfect, and he should then perform on wild birds just as he does with pigeons. However, I think that after two weeks or so of training with the use of pigeons, it is better to continue the training with game birds, so that the dog will know the scent of game birds, and become familiar with their activities in the wild state.

Possibly the dog has come along so well that you are tempted to put him aside to wait until you can put the finishing touches on him during hunting season under actual hunting conditions. However, this isn't very practical, since there are so many distractions in the hunting field that you can never really handle the dog as he should be handled. A natural setting creates problems which you are unable to control, and conditions which permit the dog freedom from strict compliance with what he has learned. Thus, much of the training you have already accomplished will go down the drain.

To use pen-raised quail you will need to build the comeback pen which is described in detail in the appendix. Working a dog on quail is somewhat different from work with pigeons. You will be unable to exercise complete control over him at all times unless you keep constant restraint on him with the check cord, and this hampers his hunting far enough from you to find enough birds to do a good day's work.

With the check cord attached to his collar, lead the dog to a spot some distance from the quail pen, but close enough for him to see the quail as they are released. (You have previously released the quail a number of times, and they are already trained to return to the pen.)

Of course, you never allow the dog to come close enough to the quail pen to be able to see the quail inside and point them. This is

Five-week-old pointer puppies pointing harnessed quail. It is apparent that puppies of this age do not have eyesight or scenting ability to any great degree but they do point. This is the first time these puppies ever smelled quail. Training should start early.

an unnatural condition, and you should always strive for natural conditions like those you would encounter during open hunting season.

When the dog can observe the flight of the birds he will be more anxious to reach the area where they settle down and to search for them, and he will learn to mark them down. However, you should always be deliberate when working a dog, so don't rush to the spot where the birds went down. Walk the dog in another direction and allow some time to elapse before you take him to the vicinity of the birds. In addition, when birds are flushed they become air-washed, and there is little scent for the dog to smell. After a time the body scent will return and scenting conditions will return to normal. A dog with a superb nose cannot point a bird if there is no scent. Many novice trainers become disappointed with their dog under such circumstances, but it is not the dog's fault. He does not point the bird unless he sees it, but he does point birds by scent, and he cannot point something that doesn't exist.

Keep the check cord attached to his collar until he locates and points a few birds. If he does a good job with no mistakes, drop the check cord and let him work with it trailing, if he will. This will permit you to retain some measure of control and he will realize he is not entirely on his own, which will make him handle more kindly. If he makes intentional mistakes, hold the check cord in your hand

The stake will prove of great assistance when you want to flush a bird without interference from the dog.

again and restrain him until he finds some more birds and points them stanchly.

After a time, remove the check cord again. When he points a bird, walk up to him, and with a show of confidence stoop down to his level and pet him. Talk to him in low tones and tell him he is a good dog. Make it appear by your actions and the tone of your voice that you are pleased with him, regardless of your true feeling. Lift him by his tail, catching hold of it close to his body; hold him in this position a few seconds, then gently lower him to the ground. Gently push on his rear end. He will allow you to push him until he falls heels over head before he will let himself be forced into the birds. Do it just as you did when working with the pigeon.

Praising the dog when he does a piece of good work is of such vital importance to successful training that it cannot be overemphasized or mentioned too often. It definitely induces the dog to want to do your bidding, and he will learn much faster if you will do your part as it should be done.

Let him stand on point for five minutes or so while you make much of him. His joy will know no bounds, for what could be sweeter than having the effluvia of game birds in his nostrils, while having the boss making such a fuss over him? Finally, walk in front of him and flush the bird. If you were shooting to kill, this would equal open-season hunting, the real thing. There can be no improvement on this type of training.

Let the dog find some more singles. Repeat the procedure of handling him, and don't forget to be lavish with the praise. If you are working only one dog, let him find and point birds as long as he shows interest. The very young dog may tire after a time, but it isn't likely that an older dog will ever tire. What does happen, though, is that eventually the birds become widely scattered and air-washed from so many flights, and it becomes difficult for the dog to locate them.

Let me warn you about another thing: Many times a covey of birds, when flushed, will settle down in an open field where cover is very sparse. You will feel confident that your dog will find and point every bird, but even though he covers ground where you know the birds are, time and again, he cannot find one bird; neither can you flush one. This is one of the secrets of nature. Quail know where this condition exists, and they know the exact plot of ground where it exists. Of course, that is why they sometimes fly to an open area that has no overhead cover to protect them against airborne predators.

At times, pen-reared quail when released will run and scatter in all directions, and the young dog, inexperienced as he is, will have great difficulty in locating them. He will make many points on ground scent, which must be expected until he learns the difference between ground scent and body scent.

When training a number of dogs, the procedure is the same as when training one dog.

Beautiful style on pen-reared quail.

However, it will save time and steps if you can take all the dogs to the training area, tie them up on individual chains, and work them one at a time.

An excellent set-up is to fix a chain between two trees or posts, and fasten to it drop chains about fifteen inches long, placed four feet apart. (This is a sufficient distance to prevent the dogs from making contact with each other and fighting.) Snap a drop chain to each dog's collar and you are ready for the day's work.

I prefer working dogs in this manner. It is less time-consuming, and all the dogs get an education from watching each other go through the routine of training.

When you are working with a number of dogs, it is a great help if there is a pond located nearby where the dogs can drink. Otherwise you must have a fairly large container and carry the water to the training area. With the hot weather, and the excitement of training, the dogs soon become hot, and their scenting ability will suffer if they do not have water.

Shooting Over the Dog

I believe that all of us, at one time or another, have been tormented by the thought of what might have been. Don't ever let this happen because of your haste to test your good, young dog's reaction to gunfire. Never let yourself get into the position where you will be compelled to say in retrospect, "If only I had not been so impetuous."

Up to this point, we have not shot a gun over the young dog, purposely awaiting the opportune moment, for in my opinion, it is unwise to shoot over a dog until he has retrieved a bird or two. Now that he has retrieved birds, the time is ripe.

Since shooting over a dog and retrieving go together, I like to use pigeons for the dog's in-

After the dog has been shot over a few times with the pistol muzzle held to the ground it is safe to shoot with the muzzle held high in the air. This gives a much louder report. Be sure the dog is on the move to retrieve when you fire the gun. Should the dog be without interest when you fire it will likely frighten him.

troduction to gunfire. The procedure I use is as follows: First, I get an assistant and equip him with a .22 starter's pistol, or a rifle or revolver, loaded with blank ammunition. Since the first shots are so critical, I warn him to point the muzzle of the gun toward the ground so that the sound will be muffled, and tell him to be certain not to fire until the dog is on the move after the bird has moved and his attention is on it. (I think that firing a gun while the dog is standing idle is completely unnatural, and nothing is better calculated to make him afraid of gunfire.)

I then plant a pigeon which has had its flight feathers pulled, as described earlier, and station the assistant about twenty-five yards away. I lead the dog upwind of the bird and let him point it. Then I remove the check cord or drop it and I walk up and disturb the pigeon, getting it to flutter away. As soon as the dog starts running eagerly after the pigeon, I signal the assistant to fire the blank, while carefully observing the dog. The chances are he won't even notice the discharge. However, if he stops and/or throws his head in the air, it indicates that he doesn't like gunfire very much, and is a warning to proceed with extreme caution.

When he will immediately go after the pigeon to retrieve it, paying no attention to gunfire from the .22, hold the muzzle of the gun high in the air. This will cause the report to be louder.

After firing over the dog often enough to be

sure he has no fear of the mild report of the
.22 blank, you can then use the .410 or the
20-gauge shotgun. If he shows the slightest
fear when you fire the larger-bore gun, omit
the firing until he regains confidence or go
back to using the .22. Go through the same
precautions with the larger-bore gun that you
did with the .22.

Dogs better understand things done in a
natural manner, so never fire the gun until the
bird has been flushed. This, of course, is the
way it is done under actual hunting conditions. And later on, in fairness to the dog, and
to help him observe the rules you have spent
long hours in teaching him, refrain from firing
at wild-flushing birds during open shooting
season; shoot only at birds which the dog has
pointed.

Steady to Wing and Shot

At this point, your dog will point stanchly, retrieve without hesitation, and has been shot
over enough times to ensure that he will not
become gun-shy, and the time has come to
kill some birds over him. Before we start,
however, you have a decision to make. Do
you want him to be steady to both wing and
shot, or only steady to wing?

Dogs that have been taught to retrieve will
instinctively take off with the shot to fetch
birds that may fall to the gun. They are difficult to restrain, especially if they see the
bird fall, and this is understandable. You must

decide if you prefer your dog to remain steady on point to wing and shot, or if you prefer to let him break shot to retrieve. You will experience no difficulty in getting him to break shot, but if you want him to be steady both to wing and shot, you must keep the check cord on him and force him to stand until given the command "Fetch." In a short while you can have him standing steady to wing and shot with no means of restraint except "Whoa," until you walk up to him and touch him lightly on the head, which is the signal for him to retrieve or resume hunting. If he is to retrieve, of course, he must be told by saying, "Dead bird, fetch."

The class bird dog that is steady both to wing and shot will make the biggest impression on those who witness his performance, for it is the mark of the finished shooting dog; a dog trained by a finished trainer. Of course when hunting a dog that is steady to wing and shot with dogs that are not, it will be quite a problem to restrain him, for it is a lot to expect of a dog that loves to retrieve to stand steady time after time while other dogs do all the retrieving. Many times you will hear people say, "Don't hunt your finished dog with dogs that are not steady to wing and shot." That's like saying "Hunt by yourself."

Moreover, the shooting dog that is not steady to wing and shot will be in a position to catch many crippled birds that might otherwise escape.

All upland game can run faster than a man

A solid point and honor on a pigeon.

if there are trees and underbrush for them to duck around when you get close to them. And even an experienced dog often has difficulty in catching a crippled bird. A wing-tipped quail can put a lot of distance between the spot where he fell, apparently stone cold dead, and the spot where he will be found, in a very few minutes. If a dog is compelled to stand on point until permitted to break to retrieve, the quail will have a head start and this will put the dog at such a disadvantage that many crippled birds will be lost.

On the other hand, steady to wing and shot is the hallmark of the high-class dog—the most impressive to watch, the most credit to the trainer. Since there's nothing to explain about letting a dog break to wing and shot, I'll go ahead and tell you how to train him not to.

Select another pigeon. Do not pull its flight feathers. Hold the pigeon in your hand and "rock" it to make it dizzy. This is accomplished by swinging your arm around in a fast, short circular motion, much like wringing a chicken's neck, except that you hold the bird by its body instead of the head. Hook your index finger over the pigeon's wing to prevent the bird from sliding out of your hand. You will soon learn how many circular motions to make, depending on how long you want the pigeon to remain on the ground before it stirs. (If you make it very dizzy, it will remain without stirring for as long as half an hour, perhaps longer, but you will never need this much unless you are testing the dog's stanchness.)

At this point we make a change in the way we have been proceeding. What you now want is for the dog to point the bird stanchly, and hold steady for the flush and shot as you wish him to under actual hunting conditions. If you are working without a helper, you now have both hands full, for handling the dog on the check cord and shooting the bird takes a bit of doing. However, after a few days of practice, everything will run smoothly.

The stake which you have driven into the ground will be your helper. Wrap the check cord around the stake one half-turn so that the dog can be restrained when the bird is flushed until you release him with the command "Dead bird, fetch." Try not to become excited when firing live ammunition, even though the pigeon is a fast flier and you must generally shoot very quickly. Let me warn you that if the dog hits the check cord at the same time you fire the gun, it can jerk your gun down until it points at the dog. So make certain that the pigeon is high enough in the air to avoid any possibility of danger to the dog. Some dogs will stand erect on their hind feet to observe the flight of the pigeon or the quail, and this puts them in a dangerous position, too.

When you fire the gun and, you hope, drop the bird, release the check cord from the stake and command the dog, "Dead bird, fetch." Having hit the end of the check cord a few times, the dog will have learned just how far he can go, and he will stop short of the end of it if he feels the least restraint, so you must give him sufficient slack so that he will feel free. It may take a trial or two, but it won't be long until he will go all the way to the bird.

Should he run all the way to the bird, or to the end of the check cord, without the command "Dead bird, fetch," it is a good time to up-end him to remind him that he must perform on command only. If he continues to hit the end of the check cord without command, give him a little punishment, remembering to give him a sound petting after the punishment. The petting will restore the dog's confidence and affection for you, and yet he will continue to associate his misbehavior with the punishment.

A reminder for those who doubt the intelligence of a dog: An intelligent dog will soon learn not to break at flush or shot when the check cord is attached to his collar, but will break every time when the means of restraint is removed. As smart as the dog is, the trainer can go him one better and use two check cords, a heavy one and a light one. Unsnap the heavy check cord, making as much noise with the snap as possible by letting go with a metallic click of the snap spring a number of times, and he will assume you have removed the check cord, which you have. He will go with the flush and shot, only to discover, too late, that he has been fooled when he hits the end of the light check cord. This is more than he can figure out, and he will be more hesitant about giving it another trial.

The trainer must always wear a heavy leather glove on the hand that handles the check cord. The glove will protect the hand from rope burns and loss of skin. Dogs with great desire will hit the end of the check cord with such vigor, and hit it so often, that the man holding the check cord will be thankful when the dog has had enough.

Another point of vital importance to remember when training dogs: Always make certain the check cord is in front of you. Never allow it to become wrapped around your body. If it is in front of you at all times, there will be no danger that the dog will hit the end of it when you are not watching him, pulling your arm behind you and twisting your arm. A sixty-pound dog running at full throttle is a force to be respected, quite capable of breaking your arm.

We have now progressed with the dog's training to the point where he will point stanchly, hold steady to point for command to retrieve, and do a fair job of retrieving, and he has been shot over a sufficient number of times with the different calibers of guns. Now all we need do is continue his training until he is ready for opening day of quail season.

When you take him hunting, you will know a proud moment when he points his first covey of birds and performs like a finished shooting dog—and you realize that you alone are responsible for his finished performance.

Handling the Dog in the Hunting Field

I can't deny that there is one dog in ten thousand that can virtually train himself, just by going hunting, without the benefit of any preliminaries. But they're so darn rare, I certainly wouldn't bother to wait to run into one. It's a whole lot more practical to get a pup of good stock, give him every fair chance to learn his job, and then put him in the hunting field and let him finish his education.

I don't think anyone can deny that there is no substitute for shooting birds over a dog's points in the hunting field to finish him as a dog. No training-field or game-farm simulation can ever be quite the same, or provide the same wealth of experience on where to find birds and how to handle them in their native habitat. Thus the main thing, once the open season comes on, is to take your dog afield often enough, and give him a chance to put his instincts and training to work without handling him to death. He won't do everything right the first time, but give him a chance to develop his own specialized skills without too much intervention on your part.

Similarly when you own a dog that is thoroughly finished on game birds, one that can be depended upon to do a workmanlike job every day, it is best to let him handle birds in his own fashion. Anyhow, I doubt that you or I could give such a dog any instruction that would improve on his own effort. His hunting instincts, his experience and intelligence, tell him how to look for birds and where they are most likely to be found.

When a dog finds birds and is flagging on point (wagging his tail), which indicates indecision as to their exact location, never whoa him, but urge him on to pinpoint the location. I would rather see a dog flush birds on occasion than have him putter around on ground scent.

The hard-working bird dog that covers a lot of ground at a fast pace must have a good nose to suit his speed, or he will accidentally flush many birds. When first put down, some dogs are full of run for the first hour or so, and never seem to get their noses synchronized with the speed.

A dog with a good nose will not putter around on ground scent but will circle when he first scents birds. He has great confidence in his scenting ability and because of such confidence will handle birds in a bold manner. The dog that seeks body scent only will find the birds and point them before the ground scenter has fully determined that it is bird scent he has discovered.

I recently hunted with a friend who owned a ground-scenting dog. As we walked along, my friend said, "He has struck a track." His words reminded me of the words used by hound-dog men when one of their hounds open on the hot track of a fox or coon. "Just wait a minute and he will track the birds up," he said. We waited, while the dog, nose to the ground, trailed the birds for the better part of two hundred yards. Finally he stopped, lifted his head as if completely bewildered, switched ends and tracked back to the starting point by the same route. All the while, he had been backtracking the birds!

He did manage to find the birds, but another dog had been pointing them all the time he had been tracking. He tracked up to the pointing dog, passed him, and only then did he establish point. My friend said he thought it was an intelligent piece of work on his dog's part. He didn't fault his dog for tracking the birds or stealing the point of another dog! It takes all kinds.

When scenting conditions are poor, a dog with the best nose may be compelled to put his nose to the ground for faint bird scent, but he will keep his nose on the ground only long enough to be certain it is bird scent he smells. He will then circle, testing the air currents for body scent. This is the mark of an intelligent dog.

When birds are nervous and running from a dog, if he is the brainy type of dog he will also circle the birds, cut them off and force them to hold to point. Only the dog of experience and intelligence will circle birds in this fashion, but all dogs should be encouraged to do so. However, there are many hunters who consider this show of intelligent bird handling a fault, and will not permit their dog to do it. This is a simple case of overhandling—a foolish man attempting to show an intelligent dog how to do his work.

Last season I was hunting a good pointer. He made a wide cast up a barren fence row. The thought entered my head that he was wasting time when the dog roaded and came to a statuesque point. It looked so foolish that I felt certain he had an unproductive point, although the dog was not given to unproductives. When I walked in front of him, totally unprepared, a large covey took wing. The dog gave me quite a look when he was not called upon to retrieve.

When a dog is finished on game, don't rush to him when he points birds, but don't take time out to sit on a log and rest. Show him the consideration to which all good dogs are entitled. A dog that is as steady as a rock may become excited and do some flushing if you run to him when he points birds. He will be there when you arrive, so go to him at a normal walking gait.

It is not necessary to say one word to the finished dog when you approach him on point. He knows what is expected of him and he will respond to your demands if properly handled. However, the young, inexperienced dog should be approached carefully when he is pointing birds. If you caution him with "Whoa," and he flags, from then on remain quiet and perhaps he will quit flagging. While flagging is not a serious fault, it is far better if the dog does not do it, because younger dogs will sometimes move in on a flagging dog with the mistaken belief that the dog is not, in fact, pointing birds. The young dog may continue to flag if you continue to caution him, but when he is hunted day after day, he will gain confidence in his ability to handle birds and perhaps will completely stop flagging.

It is best to approach the young dog from the side where he can see you, rather than from his rear, which is the normal approach when a dog is pointing birds. When you come up to him from his rear and shoot over him, possibly directly over his head, it may cause him to leave the birds and run around to the other side so that he can see you as you approach. This is really one form of blinking.

Never chase a crippled bird unless your

dog doesn't see the running bird, and doesn't know the direction the bird has taken. Let the dog do the chasing; it is part of his work, and he gets enjoyment out of it. When you down a bird, stand where you are when you fire, and wait for the dog to retrieve it. If you rush to the spot where the bird fell and the dog has already found the bird, he may get the idea you are trying to catch him for one reason or another, and he may become excited and run away with the bird.

After he has caught the bird, if he doesn't promptly come to you, turn your back on him and walk briskly away. Many times this will cause him to come to you in a hurry.

Always let the dog try to complete his work. When he fails, then you can give him assistance. The young dog must be shown how to perform, but you should give him every opportunity to do his work in his own fashion before you interfere. Of course, his way must be the accepted manner of performance.

Constantly talking or yelling to a bird dog while he is hunting is a common fault, and a terrible habit. Shouting words which some hunters consider encouragement, and blowing the whistle every couple of minutes, will only distract the dog from his work, and in his confusion he will be unable to concentrate.

It is axiomatic that the man who talks incessantly has great difficulty in attracting a listener. The same holds true between a gunner and his dog.

The stylish dog is a joy to behold.

I recently hunted with a friend who thought he had to remind his dog that we were looking for quail by saying, "Look for 'em." I said to him, "You are wasting your dog's time; tell him to *find* 'em." I feel sure he didn't realize I meant to criticize his unnecessary instructions, which, of course, were completely ignored. The dog was diligently searching for birds, and he would have found them just as soon as he could without near-constant chatter from his owner.

Constant talk, yelling and blowing the whistle will, in time, cause the dog to turn a deaf ear to it, and he will eventually, perhaps in disgust, pay not the slightest attention to the whistle or to the man blowing it. Put yourself in your dog's position. How would you like to be interrupted every few seconds?

When your dog makes a cast looking for birds, he doesn't expect to be stopped, his cast half completed, by the whistle. He should be allowed to go all the way, not compelled to abandon his birdy objective, which may lie at the end of the cast. He has sized up his cast before he started it; he visualized how far he intended to go, and where he was most likely to find a covey of birds, and if he is permitted to complete his mission, will either find the birds or return to check with you when it is completed. Can you find fault with such sensible reasoning on the dog's part? This is what is known as having "bird sense," which I could never find much reason to fault.

Retriever field-trial trainers make extensive use of the whistle, and teach their dogs to understand and obey a surprising number of different signals. I don't think the average upland hunter or pointer trainer needs to concern himself with any such fancy system of whistles, because for him, the whistle's main use is simply to attract the dog's attention and/or to let him know where his owner is. If blowing a whistle serves no purpose except to let the dog know where you are, obviously it should be avoided unless the dog is lost. If the dog hears the whistle periodically he needn't bother to keep the hunter's position in mind and won't bother to come in to check on his whereabouts. Moreover, a dog can't do a good job of hunting if he is constantly bothered by the sound of the whistle. In time, many will learn to ignore the whistle and tend to become self-hunters, checking in only occasionally.

For all of this, the first few times you take the young dog afield, he will be lost most of the time. Though the whistle will be useful in helping him to locate you, do not use it more than absolutely necessary; just give it a couple of blasts when it is evident that he is lost. (Later on I'll tell you what to do about the dog who knows darn well where you are, but doesn't care.)

IV

Correcting Faults

Discipline and Punishment

I have already dealt with the subject of correction in relation to the dog's early training. If the "stitch in time" is taken intelligently, the novice owner will not find too many difficult problems to handle with the mature dog. In practice, however, the amateur trainer is still likely to encounter some stubborn problems that do not respond to ordinary treatment, and the professional is certain to encounter them with older dogs. In fact, out of the average group of a dozen dogs in a professional trainer's kennels, the chances are that almost every one of them will fit into one or more of the following canine problem categories, and the trainer is expected to correct them all:

The dog that flushes birds
The dog that won't honor a bracemate's point
The dog that mutilates birds (or eats them)
The dog that won't come when called
The dog that won't whoa
The dog that chases farm animals
The dog that picks fights with other dogs
The dog that only hunts for himself
The dog that won't do *anything* he doesn't want to do

These are difficult problems to solve, but they can be solved, and believe me, you think much more of the dog when they have been solved. Unfortunately, however, you can't solve them just by telling the dog to "cut that out!" Despite all the varied opinions, there is just one way to solve these problems, only one plausible answer: by punishing the dog when he does wrong and knows it.

It's very much like bringing up children. The "spare-the-rod-and-spoil-the-child" approach can be overdone, and pains must be taken to ensure that the punishment fits the crime, but how many well-behaved children (or dogs) do you know that never felt a whack?

Most faults result from a breakdown in the dog's obedience, from a failure of discipline.

Discipline is basically rule or system applied to action; it is training which corrects, molds, strengthens or perfects. Punishment is a means of making discipline effective. It is a penalty inflicted on an offender as retribution or, in our case, as a means of reformation and prevention.

It is of extreme importance that the trainer learn how to correct dogs through punishment that is rational, just and unemotional. You must never let mood dictate punishment. Just because you are in a good frame of mind, do not dispense with punishment. By the same token, if you are down in spirit, don't punish the dog because of the fact. It is far better to forget training altogether on days when you are feeling low.

With almost every hunter, the dog is more likely to be punished for misbehavior if shooting is slow and the bag of birds is slow in coming. It isn't difficult for a dog to get away with infractions of the rules when a bird falls to the gun each time the gun is fired. Yet the gunner's jovial or petulant mood should not be allowed to determine whether or not to punish the dog.

Never administer punishment for unintentional misbehavior, but never permit a dog to evade punishment when he knowingly and flagrantly commits misbehavior. Indiscriminate punishment is worse than none and must be avoided.

Perhaps to the uninitiated, it may seem that I am placing too much stress on punishment, but it must be so for the very important reason that you must face the fact that it just isn't possible to train a dog without resorting to punishment.

A dog's mission in life is to hunt—to find game birds, and to handle them correctly. So why permit the dog to fritter away his life and never know the joys of accomplishing his mission, or the pleasures of receiving the red-carpet treatment that is accorded to the virtuoso shooting dog? It is so unfair to the dog. He can accomplish little without assistance from man. He must be shown by man. Give this matter some thought and you will realize this statement is nothing more than common sense, which must be a considered factor in all phases of training the bird dog.

Complete absence of punishment will let the dog know he has no reason to change his self-styled manner of performance and all training attempts may wind up a complete fiasco, but if you will do your duty to the dog, you will sense a feeling of overwhelming wonder when he finally performs to perfection and reaches the zenith of his potential. But it will be a frosty Friday when a dog changes his manner of performance without a firm hand from his handler. Of course, while the trainer must always be firm in making the dog understand his whimsical foolishness will not be tolerated, he must not let frustration unconsciously build to the point where it may lead to punishment that is more severe than is justified.

The close friendship between man and his dog is never impaired by a firm hand, but surely will be by undeserved punishment. When you are compelled to punish a dog, if it is done in a businesslike manner his affection for you will not decrease. When you are finished with the punishment, allow equal time for petting; tell him by word and action that he is still wanted and that the bond between you and your dog is as strong as before the punishment.

Deserved punishment, applied in a sensible manner, will increase your dog's respect for you—and don't ever harbor the idea that he doesn't know if you are to be respected. There is no need to make a big deal out of punishment, to assume a blustery attitude. Do it in a quiet, dignified manner and the dog will never fear you. And let me repeat: never forget that he is entitled to be petted after punishment.

Only one man in a hundred will consider having a worthless animal put away. Most would rather give the dog to a very good friend or a brother-in-law. However, a bird dog with no value as a bird dog will seldom have a permanent home. He will be kicked around from pillar to post and his meals will be few and far between. Proper care and affection will be completely missing. It is something to remember when you are hesitant about using force to make your dog put forth his best effort. Give it some thought and you will realize there is no other way.

It is unforgiveable to make a dog cowed, and to avoid it one must consider the temperament of each individual. A dog must not have his dignity destroyed; without it he is nothing. Nothing must be done to him to discourage him from holding his head and tail high in a dignified manner. Every man would rather have a dog that is sure of himself, a bold dog; one that goes to his game and handles it with a great show of confidence, not a creeper that goes to his game while crawling along on his belly; not a ground scenter but a dog that seeks body scent only. Who wants a dog with a timorous disposition that lies down when spoken to, regardless of the evident kindness in the tone of voice?

Use of the Flushing Whip

With the young dog, a cross word and mild correction are usually enough to obtain compliance if training has been methodical, progressive and consistent. But many older dogs will frankly look to take advantage of you, over and over again, and simply ignore almost everything you do until they get good and ready. For such obdurate cases, the only real solution in the vast majority of cases is punishment he can feel, administered through the medium of the flushing whip.

The flushing whip has other uses, of course. Its primary use if for flushing birds before the dog in field trials, and it can also serve as a lead when you need to snap it to a dog's collar while crossing a road or highway on which there is dangerous traffic. But it is also a key which can unlock many doors for the trainer, a tool which can be effectively employed to encourage a strong-willed dog to observe the rules of good behavior again.

If you are of the opinion that you can be successful in training a dog without authority, do not carry a flushing whip, but if you do carry one, do not wear it solely as an ornament. The headstrong dog must learn to accept it as a badge of authority.

Most people will agree that there are very few finished shooting dogs, and a lack of force in correcting faults is probably the main reason why this is so, even though it's unfashionable to say it out loud these days. One of the few trainers who was ever brave enough to "tell it like it is" in print was Logan Bennett, who had this to say in his fine book, *Training Grouse and Woodcock Dogs* (G.P. Putnam, 1948): "I venture to say that not more than one dog in a thousand is ruined by whipping, but at least nine hundred and ninety-nine out of a thousand poor dogs are not worth having because of a lack of adequate correction. Your dog may never need many whippings — but when he needs one, be sure that he will remember it."

When using the flushing whip for punishing a dog, be careful where the blows fall. Never hit him on the head, where there would be a chance of damaging an eye. Instead, use the whip along the flank and along the back. If half a dozen strokes are not sufficient to deter misbehavior, make the punishment more severe the next time. The amount of punishment differs with every dog. The trainer/owner must know the character of the dog and punish the meek and the bold one accordingly. Also pet them and praise them according to merit.

There is no point in punishing the headstrong dog unless the punishment is sufficiently severe to leave a lasting memory. However, it is never necessary to be cruel.

Remember that dogs are great gamblers, at times taking long odds that they will get away with misbehavior with no punitive action being taken against them. In playing poker the odds against making a flush are 508 to 1 (*World Almanac*), but a dog will take such odds as long as there is any chance at all. The odds must lengthen until he realizes he has *no* chance to win.

The following illustrates the chances a bird dog will take. About two years ago I purchased a son of Wayriel Allegheny Sport, a noted field-trial champion. (Allegheny Sport had forty-nine finds in six hours in national competition, an all-time record which isn't likely to be challenged.)

The man I purchased the dog from told me the dog was finished on game, but the price was so low that I felt sure the dog was worthless. When I took him out for a trial, he hadn't been down more than five minutes when he deliberately ran through a covey of birds and chased them, giving tongue like a treeing Walker coonhound in full cry. When he returned I gave him a dose of hickory tea. Then I turned him loose and he ran through a second covey and chased them as far as he could follow their flight. Then he proceeded to put the singles to flight, one after another, until he had found and flushed the majority of the covey.

When he gave it up and returned, I was waiting for him, annoyed with the idea I had been too trusting. All the while the hickory tea had been brewing, and this time the dog got a somewhat stronger dose. After the second treatment the dog got the message and from that point on he showed me unbelievably good performance. It turned out that there was never doubt in his mind as to proper behavior, but he had to take the gamble that I was ignorant of how he should perform. Had I taken no punitive action against his flagrant disregard of manners he wouldn't have been worth the powder and shot.

Range

Perhaps a competent trainer can permanently change a dog's range, but it is my belief that it is largely an inherent trait which is difficult to alter. It might be difficult to explain what makes one dog run to the limits, while his brother or sister may be a relatively close working dog. Some authorities explain it by merely saying, "It is an inbred quality," which is just another way of saying "inherent trait."

It is my belief that it is much easier to exchange the dog than it is to alter his range. But unfortunately, when purchasing dogs, many owners give little thought to the dog's range. One of the first questions that should be settled when purchasing a dog is: "Do I want a dog that hunts all the area within a half-mile or so, or do I want a dog that hunts the close-in area only?"

Once a dog can be depended upon to handle birds in the accepted manner, I see nothing wrong with the dog ranging out for a half-mile, but when he does one must be willing, at times, to spend time looking for him when he finds birds at this distance. The average hunter does not want a dog to go so wide, and it is admittedly difficult to keep track of the wide-going dog when hunting in woodland or dense undergrowth areas where he will be out of sight most of the time. Even so, if he is endowed with intelligence he will usually alter his range and hunt to the gun under these conditions. If you are partial to the dog that is never out of sight, the average pointer or setter may be a poor choice as a shooting dog unless you go out of your way to find one that will hunt a very close pattern.

Many excellent prospects, and finished shooting dogs as well, are disposed of because of their excessively wide hunting pattern. It may be the only criticism of the dog's performance, but instead of making a real effort to control the wide-going dog, many owners would rather exchange him for a dog with a more restricted hunting pattern and hence less bird-finding potential.

Of course, the wide-ranging dog must be controllable or he leaves much to be desired as a shooting dog. With the dog of uncontrollable disposition, it takes an experienced handler to get good performance from him, and he is more than the average man can handle.

It seems strange, but one of the best ways to deal with the wide-running dog that does not want to hunt to the gun and keep a check on the owner's whereabouts is to climb a tree and hide from him. It takes a lot of patience, but it works.

When you are hidden from his view and

A far-out find.

finally see him coming in your direction, looking for you, make no sound that will let him know where you are. Let him run past the tree where you are concealed and go on for some distance; you'll see him stop and listen for any sound that will tell him where you are. He is confident that you are nearby, or he would not remain in the immediate area and look for you. But he can't figure out where you could have gotten to in such a short interval of time. He'll become worried and frustrated when he is unable to locate you, for all dogs, especially those with a tractable disposition, have a great fear of becoming lost.

When he goes by your hiding place again and it appears he has decided you are not near, let him move on for a hundred yards or so. Then when he stops and is listening for sound from you, give a low toot on the whistle, loud enough for him to hear, but not loud enough for him to get an exact fix on your position. He will come your way again, go some distance in the opposite direction, stop, look and listen again.

Let him fret. The more he frets, the less you will have to, later on. When he continues his search going away from you, give another low toot on the whistle to get him to change direction again and come in your direction. Give him more cause for worry. Remember, the lesson is for the dog, not you, so don't feel sorry for him. Keep it up until you feel that he has had enough to make him want to hunt to the gun. If it doesn't prove to be a lasting lesson to him, do it another time.

Let the dog continue the fruitless search as long as he remains in sight of your hiding place without prompting from the whistle. Usually, he will not look up in the tree where you are until he detects the source of the whistle sound. The longer it takes him to find you, the happier he will be when he does find you, and the longer he will remember the lesson.

Never try hiding from more than one dog at the same time. If you do, both dogs will either run out of range of the sound of the whistle or will pay little attention to the whistle, and nothing will be accomplished.

This procedure will not work on every dog. If the dog does not have affection for his owner, it will do little to make him keep a periodic check on the owner's whereabouts. But it does work wonders with some dogs.

The Fighter

Many dogs are antisocial and always looking for an opportunity to fight with any dog put down in the field with them. In many cases this is caused by jealousy, perhaps brought on by fear their bracemate will find birds ahead of them. Though many owners ignore it, this is a serious fault and every effort must be made to curb such aggressiveness. Why does a dog owner allow, or even encourage, his dog to fight with other dogs? There can be no sensible reason for it. Perhaps they think it is a way of saying "My dog is better than your dog," but it's a poor one.

When a dog fights with other dogs he must be punished, and the punishment must be increasingly severe on each occasion. If an owner had a few hundred dollars invested in a dog, he would think twice before allowing his dog to fight. The $10 dog is more likely to be allowed to fight.

Dogs are extremely jealous of each other. Some may want to fight with a dog that is receiving petting, or if present when a dog is punished, may want to assist in the punishment. To permit this conduct will contribute to the fighter's desire to fight with any and all dogs, and in time he will become so belligerent it will be impossible to hunt him with other dogs. He will become so obsessed with the desire to fight that he will not permit another dog to ride in a car with him. Even if he never wins a fight, he will always be willing to keep trying, perhaps in the hope that one day he will find a dog that knows less about fighting than he does.

The fighter must be severely punished each time he attacks another dog. Token punishment will not deter the fighter from repeated misbehavior. If the punishment is not severe, and does not leave a lasting memory, there is no point in punishing at all.

Each time the fighter shows a desire to fight by growling at other dogs and raising the hair along his back, give him a whack with the flushing whip. Should he attack another dog, take hold of his collar and strike him on the back and along the flank with the flushing whip until he releases his hold and backs off. Then continue the punishment until you think he has had enough.

If you can't separate the fighting dogs with the flushing whip, lift the ear of the aggressor and yell loudly in his ear. When all other efforts fail, this will usually cause him to release his hold on the other dog.

Should one of the dogs accidentally bite you, it seldom will break the skin. The dog will realize he has made a mistake and let go without doing any real harm.

However, I have seen dogs that would constantly keep their owners on the defensive in fear of getting bitten. This is caused by the owner's failure to let the dog know who is the boss.

Seldom will a dog, however mean he may be, bite his master. The dog usually knows when he can get away with it. Such behavior must be dealt with at the outset, and when the dog realizes what to expect when he does it, he will not try it a second time.

The Self-Hunter

Many dogs have a tendency to hunt by themselves, out of sight and control of the handler. The longer they are permitted to do this the more difficult it is to change their self-styled hunting pattern. A dog of this trait never seems to have a care about anything or any-body. He will become very independent and an excellent bird finder, but if he is to become a dependable shooting dog, he must be taught to hunt to the gun. Once he becomes confirmed in his hunting habits, his affection for his owner dwindles. All he needs his owner for is to take him to and from the hunting area. He would as soon hunt for one person as another, and he will leave his owner and go to another hunter, a total stranger, when he hears distant gunfire. All the care and affection you may bestow upon him will not alter his feeling for you. He doesn't care where you are, although he generally knows, and you seldom know his where-abouts. Never blow the whistle when hunting a dog of this disposition, for if you do he will be in no hurry to come to you.

It generally takes drastic action to change this type of dog's hunting pattern. Perhaps the quickest way is to give him a few shocks with a remote-control shock collar, as dis-cussed in greater detail at the end of this part. When shocked by the unit, most dogs will hurry back to their owner for protection from they don't know what, and they will hesitate to get out there again, where that dreadful something attacks them. Whatever happens, the shock cannot make the situation worse. If you can't control your dog, you'd be just as well off without one.

Another type of self-hunter is the dog that will run a straight line for possibly a half-mile, never looking in your direction to discover where you might be headed. After an hour's absence, he may swing in close enough to be able to identify you, and then take off again for another distant horizon, on another absence of perhaps even longer duration. Making him subservient to the gun is a difficult undertaking, and a limit of birds is hard to come by when hunting a dog of this temperament. If you can refrain from letting him know your whereabouts, it may help, as with the bolter, to curb his desire to run, but as a general rule more drastic means must be resorted to.

It is difficult to be satisfied with a dog that is always underfoot, but even he might be preferable to one you seldom see when hunting with him. I would prefer a dog with a modest range that found only two coveys and handled them in good fashion, to a dog that found twice as many birds while hunting out of control. Control is one thing a dog must observe if one is to have an enjoyable hunt with him. The harvesting of birds without good dog performance is poor sport. If I want meat, I find that it is much cheaper to go to the market.

A Case History: Beau Jack

Four years ago I purchased a beautiful male setter with an all-white body and a black head. He bears a great resemblance to Sport's

Wonsover Beau Jack.

Peerless Pride, and Sport's name does appear on Jack's pedigree.

At the time, the dog was two years of age—a self-hunter with little regard for anything except finding birds and chasing them into the next county. I could never reach him while he was on point, and after he had flushed the birds he would not come to me, or allow me to catch him. He made a game of it. There was nothing I could do, and it didn't take long for me to find it out. I hunted him for seven days straight and not once was I able to do anything about his utter disregard for me or anything that might interfere with his enjoyment. I was determined to persevere and to make a good shooting dog of him. I wanted to hunt him whenever possible and to finish him as quickly as possible because of his advanced age, but he had other ideas. At the time I didn't know, but finishing him was to prove easy.

He finally made the mistake of allowing me to catch him. I was exceptionally fond of him — his style, beauty, intelligence and character. During the seven frustrating days I continually reminded myself not to let pent-up emotion dictate his eventual punishment, and when the time came, I was successful in controlling my urge to be severe. Instead, I gave him mild punishment and severe petting.

Did it pay off? All he ever needed was to be shown that I would not tolerate such flagrant misbehavior.

He is six years old now. That one time is the only time he has been punished. I have not seen him flush a bird intentionally since that day four years ago. It seems astounding, but he knew what to do all the time. Where he made his big mistake was in not taking into account that I also knew how he was supposed to do the job. Had he not been punished, even mildly — well, you can draw your own conclusions.

The Bolter

The bolter is more than the average owner can cope with, and sometimes even a handler with lifelong experience has great difficulty in curbing a bolter's undeniable desire to run. His urge to find birds compels him to run at breakneck speed, hour after hour, day after day. He has no intention of staying with his owner. He finds many birds which he promptly flushes and chases into the next township, for his stamina usually matches his desire to run.

Frankly, while there are a number of things which can be done in the attempt to make the dog more biddable, none will work on every dog. For the dog that isn't completely imbued with an all-consuming desire to run, attach a rubber ball to his collar, suspended by a short length of rope. This will slow him down. The rope will wrap around his legs, the ball will hit him in the stomach and on the head, and will keep him worried about where it will strike next.

For the bolter that slows down for nothing, more drastic measures must be taken. If he is made to drag or carry a heavy load, it won't take as long to wear him down. Put a harness on him with heavy chains attached, the weight of which must be determined by the dog's size and determination to run, or let him drag a heavy chain. After an hour or so of burning up energy while transporting the added weight, he will be more willing to hunt at a much slower pace, and hunt to the gun. With his energy, if only one could control it, what a bird dog the average bolter would become! Unfortunately, many never make it.

The Gun-Shy Dog

The gun-shy dogs, the bolters, and the blinkers are usually too much for the novice trainer to cope with and should ordinarily be left to a professional trainer with the necessary experience.

Many years ago I hunted with a friend who took a six-month-old puppy that had never been outside of his kennel. At the first volley of gunfire the young dog ran away. The following day he took another puppy from the same litter. The same thing happened to this one. He left them both in the field.

It is incredible, but nevertheless true, that hunters with many years of hunting experience often take young dogs hunting that have never heard the report of gunfire. Apparently they believe a bird dog is bred with a built-in "no fear" of gunfire.

As I write this I own a high-class female pointer who is both gun-shy and bird-shy. I have been working her for six months. I can shoot a 20-gauge shotgun over her five or six times and she pays little attention, but a few more shots will cause her to become afraid and she will drop her tail. If I continue to shoot, she comes to me and follows along behind me for a time; then she will resume hunting. If she were not such a beautiful dog with such outstanding potential I would never have spent so much time with her. Of late, when she points a bird, I pick her up bodily, walk up close to the bird (which I generally can see on the ground), and throw her in on the bird, at times causing the bird to flush under her stomach. This treatment seems to do her more good than having a bird flush fifteen feet or so from her, because it puts her closer to the noise. If the bird does not flush, she immediately establishes a picturesque point again. Sometimes she now attempts to catch the birds when they flush and is chasing them a short distance. With all her fear she does retrieve. I will allow her to chase birds until she is completely cured of shyness, then I will stanch her up again. At times, the trainer must create situations which produce faults in order to overcome more serious faults.

The correction of a gun-shy dog sometimes comes as a bonus from working him with a group of dogs. Presence at the training sessions is all that is required of him for the first two weeks or so, depending on how long it takes the gun-shy dog's interest and desire to develop. From watching the other dogs perform, the gun-shy dog learns that there is nothing to fear, and this helps to overcome his own fear.

Tie any gun-shy dogs at one end section of the chain where they will be out of the way. For a time they are to be observers only. They get no opportunity to perform until they show they are ready. It is amazing how quickly they lose their shyness. They sense that the other dogs have no fear and gain confidence in themselves from that fact.

At the start of the gun-shy dog's training, he

This dog is gun-shy, but she cannot resist the inherent urge to point quail.

will have no interest in anything connected with birds of any species, but when he does lose his fear, a noticeable change will take place in his actions. I sometimes think he realizes he is completely dependent upon the trainer for assistance in overcoming his fear, and learns to pay strict attention. When cured, he is often extremely cautious when working birds; though by cautious, I don't necessarily mean a creeper or plodder. But seldom will he accidentally flush a bird, and never intentionally. Should a reformed gun-shy dog become lost on point, you may as well start looking for him, for he will never leave point regardless of how many times you may blow the whistle. Any trainer will feel a sense of accomplishment when he can take one of the raff of dog society and transform him into an excellent shooting dog.

At the start of training, the gun-shy dog will usually go to any extreme to avoid witnessing the training activities. He will hide his head behind a tree and would hide behind a blade of grass if he thought it would afford him protection from the noise of the gun and the sight of birds. He dreads the sound of whirring wings, the prelude to the dreadful noise of gunfire. He can hardly avoid the noise, but he feels that if he can hide his head, it will be easier to endure.

Let the gun-shy dogs be mere spectators, day after day, never giving them an opportunity to work until they show profound interest in the work of other dogs and it becomes apparent they have overcome a great deal of their fear. You will be forewarned when they are ready for work. They will sit up, out in the open, as near to the training activities as their chain will permit, whereas just a few days earlier they would stay as far removed from the activities as their chain would permit. They will watch the trainer intently as he walks out to plant a pigeon, with no show of fear, and no attempt to run or hide. They will not duck their head or flinch when the gun is fired. These indications show that they are ready to take their turn, though in some cases they are still not as fearless as they believe. Some must spend more time on the chain after their first trial, but in the end, all of them will pass the test.

From the start of training, non-gun-shy dogs will bark furiously when you walk toward them upon returning from planting a bird. After a week or so the gun-shy dog joins in on the barking, in his desire to be a participant. It is a pathetic situation, yet somehow amusing. It will make any trainer anxious to give each one his chance to pass the test as soon as possible. Talk to them, tell all the dogs to hold on, give each one a reassuring pat on the head, and make the next selection.

All dogs will remain very quiet as you walk to the area where you intend to plant the next bird; then there is an uproar when you again walk in their direction to select the next dog to perform. Time after time, it is repeated. At any other time the loud barking would become annoying, but in this instance, it is a part of the game, a part of the cure. The barking is an indication of great interest, and this is a step toward the goal you are seeking. You will enjoy every minute of the impressive display and you will be gratified to see the gun-shy dogs take an active part in what is to be their life's work. Quick to learn, some of the more intelligent dogs will even hold their head still so that it is easier to unsnap the drop chain from their collar and put the check cord on.

This means of curing the gun-shy dog is the

most positive, foolproof and humane way to get the job done, and is easily accomplished if you have the proper set-up with which to work.

A gun-shy dog must be given special treatment. You must never strike him, even if he tries your patience to near exhaustion. Be deliberate in all your movements; a quick movement may be construed as intended punishment. Always speak to him in low, pleasant tones and it will help to reassure him. As in all phases of training the dog, your goal is interest in his work, and in finding the factor which will cause him to lose his fear.

Some dogs never seem to be adversely affected by gunfire from puppyhood to maturity, even if a shotshell with the maximum powder charge is used when they receive their baptism of gunfire. It is reasonable to think that some dogs' hearing is more sensitive than others, which could account for the difference in reactions to gunfire, but since nobody knows how well the individual dog can hear without a trial, common sense must be used when shooting over any dog for the first time. The best way to avoid shyness of any kind is to select a young dog who shows he does not know the meaning of fear—the bold one.

Many dog owners are too impatient to wait for the right moment to introduce their dog to gunfire, or to take intelligent precautions to preclude gun-shyness. Afterward, they assert that the dog must have been born gun-shy, though I fail to see how a dog can be gun-shy if he doesn't know what gunfire is. In my view, dogs are not born gun-shy; it is strictly a man-made fault, the price we pay for our own impatience, thoughtlessness and disregard for logic.

There are several other techniques for curing gun-shyness. Some are said to be less time-consuming, but in my opinion none is as foolproof, humane or effective as the "on-the-chain" method just described. Its only disadvantage is that only a trainer who has a number of dogs to work can apply it, and hence it is employed mostly by professionals.

A commonly recommended cure that does not involve the use of other dogs is the so-called "starvation" cure. In applying this method, the trainer fires a small-caliber gun (usually a .22 blank) over the dog each time food is placed before him. If the dog abandons the food (and they all do, for a while) the trainer removes it until the dog is hungry enough to go on eating while the gun is fired.

I have never used this method myself, but I've read and heard so much about it that I accept the fact that it can work in some cases — if the dog doesn't waste away from malnutrition in the meantime.

Another cure I've heard about is called the water cure. Some trainers consider the water cure to be a bit more humane than the starvation cure, though I'm not sure how the dogs feel about it. The water cure is accomplished by taking the gun-shy dog out in a boat and anchoring a bit offshore. When the trainer fires the .22, the dog will bail out and head for shore, but being tied to the anchored boat, he will be unable to tow it. The dog is permitted to swim until he is tired, at which point the trainer drags him back with the rope and starts all over again. The performance is repeated until the dog no longer leaves the boat when the .22 (and later, a 20-gauge and then a 12-gauge shotgun) is fired. It all sounds fine in theory, but that's as far as I go, not having had any occasion to try this technique myself.

The Bird-Shy Dog

Bird-shy dogs are generally more difficult to cure than gun-shy dogs, because the bird-shy dog has less interest in birds. The bird-shy dog has a real dread of making contact with game birds, and in many cases, because of this lack of interest in birds, will take to hunting and chasing rabbits instead. This in turn will cause him to have even less interest in birds, for the rabbit makes no noise to frighten him.

Illogically, the bird-shy dog has the idea that the quail are to be feared more than the gunfire, or perhaps senses that when the birds are flushed, the sound of gunfire is certain to follow. Of course, this is not always true but the true bird-shy dog shows fear of birds even if you carry no gun. (The gun-shy bird dog knows for sure what the gun is, as attested by the fact that when you load the gun and let the bolt slide forward with the usual noise, it is usually enough to put him on the run.)

Most competent trainers will guarantee the cure for these faults at a very reasonable charge, and they earn their money. The procedure they employ is very simple, and requires little work on their part, though to the amateur it would be a herculean task.

The cure is much easier to accomplish if you can get the shy dog to flush the birds. Of course, when this is accomplished, and the dog no longer has fear of birds, he must be cured of the faults you have encouraged him to learn.

Let me give you an example of what it took to cure one bad case I had to deal with.

Before I reached the age of twenty-five (which was somewhat longer ago than yesterday) I learned to refuse to accept "gift dogs." But Betsy was such a beautiful little female pointer that I made an exception and took the chance I could cure her of gun-shyness and bird-shyness.

It was a difficult job which I have spent many hours and hundreds of rounds of ammunition in accomplishing, but her way of going with a merry tail sticking straight up while running and pointing and her burning desire to find birds is adequate payment. She never seems to be affected by sore feet or sore muscles and can hunt every day.

When I first got her, she would show

Most bird-shy dogs associate the bird with a loud frightening noise. Forcing the bird-shy dog to hold a pigeon in his mouth will help him overcome his fear.

normal behavior at times, but after a few shots she would drop her tail and show great fear at the flush of a bird or the sight of another dog on point. I knew great disappointment on many occasions during a long, frustrating year but I could never bring myself to dispose of her.

I even tried taping two hours of firing on the skeet range and played it "to get her accustomed to gunfire" on many occasions. This did little good because with a shy dog, it takes interest to overcome fear.

When she pointed birds I picked her up bodily and threw her in on the birds. She finally started chasing the birds under these circumstances. I encouraged her to chase and to flush. One day she jumped in and caught a bird. I thought she was on the road to full recovery from shyness but the next time she located birds she blinked them. At times she would hunt for hours without showing fear, then for no apparent reason she would come to me and follow along behind, slinking like a mistreated dog.

If we were hunting near home, she would run for her kennel whenever she remembered her fear. Or if she could find the automobile, she would go to that.

I tried the starvation cure on her but after two days I realized I could not go through with it.

After seven days of hunting her I was discouraged to the point where I decided to give up. As a last resort I decided to try giving her tranquilizer pills. I gave her two pills and took her out. She hunted a beautiful pattern for an hour or so, and then took off for the kennel. I took her back and worked her on pen-reared birds and she showed no fear.

In the afternoon I took her hunting again. I gave her two pills and she got through the afternoon without leaving me until we were in sight of the automobile, when she couldn't stand it any longer.

Each time I took her hunting it was apparent she was making progress in the effort to overcome her great fear. Her interest was building daily. After another ten days' hunting she finally won her battle. Now she no longer fears either birds or gunfire. She is a bird dog.

Honoring

Human nature being what it is, most of us prefer to see our own dog do the pointing and the other fellow's dog do the honoring. However, the finished dog must be able to do both. It is not the dog's fault when he refuses to honor a bracemate. It is his owner's fault. Any dog will learn to honor with just a little pressure being brought to bear on him.

Refusal to honor can be caused by a number of things. Constantly hunting a dog by himself is one sure way to get him in the habit of not honoring. This fact alone should be cause for every hunter to own at least two good bird dogs. (Actually, it is better to own three or four, because you never know when one of possibly two of your dogs will be laid up for a few days, and you should have reserve dogs. I can think of nothing more disappointing than to find myself in the middle of hunting season with dogs which are unable to hunt.)

Another cause for refusal to honor is jealousy. I feel certain that every dog inherently knows what to do when he knows another dog is pointing birds. It becomes evident by his actions. When a dog slowly approaches a dog on point with a sort of apologetic attitude, his tail wagging, friendlylike, he knows the pointing dog has found birds. The culprit will not stop until his nose is out front of the pointing dog, and some are not content with stealing the point, but may deliberately flush the birds, even though he may be a completely finished dog when hunting by himself.

When a dog refuses to honor, he should be made to hunt with a nylon rope, about twenty feet long, attached to his collar. (Nylon will not become entangled in underbrush as easily as a cotton rope.) The trailing rope will enable you to catch him as he passes you in his attempts to steal points. As he passes you, grab the rope; wait until he hits the end of it, then give it a jerk with the weight of your body behind it, assisted by all the arm muscle you can possibly put into it, turning him end for end, if possible; at the same instant giving the command "Whoa." Say the command with authority, and he will obey.

When he again has the opportunity to honor, if he doesn't immediately stop and establish point behind the dog pointing the birds, take him some distance to the rear so as not to distract the pointing dog or dogs, and give him a little workout with the flushing whip. Then lead him up behind the pointing dog, repeat the command "Whoa," and if he doesn't honor this time, repeat the punish-

ment, but make him think the last punishment was fun, compared to what he is now
getting. It doesn't take many treatments to
cure the fault. Don't forget to praise and pet
the dog afterward, even though the misbehavior was strictly intentional.

For such flagrant disregard of proper behavior, you shouldn't have the slightest hesitation about punishing the dog. If he is intelligent, the punishment will cause him to
give the matter thought, and he will honor the
next dog, without command, as far as he can
see him on point, and be glad to do it. I know
that many dog owners shudder at the mention
of punishment. They may even say, "If I must
be cruel to my dog to get him to honor, well,
I just won't do it." But I don't consider de-
manding good performance to be cruelty.
If you want to coddle your dog, you must
be willing to settle for mediocre accomplishment. It's as simple as that.

The False Pointer

Even the best bird dog will occasionally
make a point when there are no birds in front
of him. When this happens it is called an
"unproductive" point, and is generally excused by saying, "The birds must have flown
before he established point." Many times this
is true, and I do not entirely agree with the
unwritten field-trial rule that puts a dog out of
contention after a brilliant performance because of one unproductive point, even if he
could otherwise have been the winner of the

event. A dog with a superior nose may have been able to point lingering scent of a bird which, for one reason or another, might have been flushed earlier, and which the winner may have passed by.

An occasional false or unproductive point, whichever you may choose to call it, can be excused. However, if it happens all the time, then it really is a fault which cannot be excused.

How can you tell when a point is false? If you are well acquainted with a dog you will know, sometimes by his pointing stance, sometimes by his actions, when he is false-pointing and when he has birds before him. When you feel certain he is false-pointing, walk in fairly close to him and say, "Get out of there." If he continues to false-point after you do this a few times, catch him and give him a modest treatment with the flushing whip; or, if you are reluctant to administer a little punishment, just don't bother to go to his point. Stand off some distance and watch him. When he learns he cannot fool you, that you will come to him only when he has birds, he will soon leave the point and resume hunting, and will eventually quit false-pointing.

It is worth mentioning that fear of severe punishment, applied by a trainer who doesn't know when or how to punish, can be one reason for a dog to start false-pointing. The dog will point when he doesn't know for sure if birds are before him rather than take a chance of flushing them and getting a severe beating. This is a good example of why the dog owner must know when and how to punish a dog, and never forget to pet the dog each time he is punished.

The Blinker

There are several types of blinkers. One type will establish point and remain stanch until the gunner walks up behind him, then break point, run around to the other side of the birds and re-establish point. This particular behavior is man-made. Although not an intolerable fault, it is nonetheless undesirable, because of its effect on other dogs which might be honoring. Of course, when the blinking dog makes his move, all honoring dogs are released from their obligation to honor, and are also free to move.

Two things may be the cause of a dog handling birds in this manner. One reason is severe and repeated punishments administered by someone who does not know when to stop punishing and start petting.

The other reason is shooting too close to the dog when he is on point, perhaps shooting directly over his head, especially the first time the dog ever hears the report of gunfire. After that, he is determined to see who is coming up to him from the rear, and he prefers to know when the big boom is coming, in order to get in the right frame of mind to endure the shock. He is very frightened of the report of gunfire and the sound of flushing birds.

Blinking, in any form, is thus caused by fear of the sound of flushing birds, the result of gunfire, or punishment—any one, or all three combined. In any case, it results from thoughtless and ignorant human actions. (I believe that all knowledgeable dog owners agree that a vast majority of the dog's faults are the direct results of man's mistakes.) But, regardless of who or what is at fault, man must be responsible for correcting faults. The dog cannot do it alone; he must have man's assistance to show him how to do it.

The true blinker is a dog that locates birds, flash-points or possibly doesn't point at all, and then makes a detour around the birds and resumes hunting. This is the worst form of blinking, and it is sometimes difficult to detect. This type of blinker believes the birds are responsible for the noise of gunfire, and in one sense they are. He rationalizes, "If I don't point these birds, and sneak away without disturbing them, they will not move and I will not be compelled to endure the sound of their flight and the dreadful noise of gunfire."

In practice, few blinkers are worth the effort required to correct the fault, but if a young dog has outstanding qualities in all other respects, it may be worthwhile to break him. This can be accomplished by hunting him in the company of finished dogs, and keeping him in tow with the check cord.

When another dog points, lead him up close to the scene where he can smell the birds and have a ringside seat at the show, see the flushing of the birds, the shooting and the retrieving. In time, he will overcome his fear. The time required to effect the cure will depend on the blinker's desire and interest. If he becomes deeply interested he may overcome the fear in a very short time.

The most favorable time to cure the blinker of his fault is during hunting season, though there is little pleasure for anyone in dragging a dog around the countryside on a check cord. One man alone can never handle the blinking dog and the other dogs and do any shooting. I have known a number of owners who have tried to cure blinkers and gun-shy dogs in this manner but it is hard work, and dangerous to man and dog. If the dog attempts to take off, and hits the end of the check cord at the same time the shot is fired, there is no way of controlling the direction of the shot path. Get an assistant to help you, or better yet, turn the dog over to a good professional trainer.

The Hard-Mouthed Retriever

If a dog is to be used as a retriever, the worst fault he can have is chewing and mutilating birds. It is no easy matter to break a dog of this intolerable fault. He must be watched carefully each time he makes a retrieve and the bird must be inspected to see if there are teeth marks on it, or if it has torn skin. If a good portion of the bird's skin is torn loose from the body, the body fluids will leak out and it will be unfit to eat.

The inveterate jaw clincher does not chew a bird but will clamp down on it so tightly the bird's intestines will be forced out. This can be tolerated better than the chewing, since it does little damage to the bird, but one should never permit it to go unnoticed. If this fault is not dealt with each time the dog roughs up a bird, the fault will become progressively worse, and he will eventually become a bird eater. I don't want to spend a day afield just in order to fill my dog's stomach. Anyhow, if I am looking for dog food, I would rather feed a dog a $4 steak than have him mutilate one bird.

The dog that is a quick grabber-upper may tear a bird's skin if he has to dig it out of thick grass. This can be excused to a certain degree, but must not be completely ignored. Give him some real gruff talk and let him know he is doing something of which you disapprove, and watch him closely to see that he doesn't get the idea of doing it with every bird which he is called upon to retrieve.

The best way to acquaint the confirmed bird chewer that he is doing wrong is to place his upper lips over his upper teeth and apply pressure. This must be done immediately after he has delivered the bird to hand. Pressure applied to his lips seems to point out to him the exact source of trouble and it will cause him to have second thoughts about doing it again. Apply sufficient pressure to make him glad when you release him.

If he doesn't get the message and persists, you've got to escalate the punishment. Put his neck between your legs so that you can hold him, and shut off his supply of air by clamping your hands over his mouth and nose. Hold a tight rein on him because he will buck like a wild bronco when the air supply becomes short. When he struggles violently and is gasping for breath, turn him loose, but make him realize he has had a close shave. Now before you arrive at the conclusion this kind of treatment will not be used on your dog, you must first ask this question: "Can I find a better method?" This is exceptionally rough treatment, but in my opinion it is not cruel, because you do it in an attempt to make a good dog a better dog. I can understand why the very idea of such treatment will make many dog owners bristle, but it must be done if the dog is to learn a lasting lesson. I sympathize with the dog, too, but I also sympathize with the man who must resort to this severe punishment. It is one measure of punishment that gives me a sinking feeling when I must use it, but nothing will give me a feeling of despair as quickly as a dog that chews birds.

As far as I am concerned, the fact that I want the bird for my own table does not enter into it, because I give 90 percent of all birds I harvest to the farmer on whose land I hunt, but I want the farmer to have good birds.

Only recently, a bird-dog owner told me the bird-chewing dog has a craving for meat, and the theory makes sense. He said, "I fed my dog one pound of raw hamburger, and he didn't chew a bird for a period of two weeks, then I fed him another pound of meat." If it works, what a simple method of correcting the retriever's most serious fault! However, I have a feeling that it's not that simple.

Immature quail are a constant source of trouble in the retrieving department and are the cause of many dogs becoming hard-mouthed. They are very tender and it is almost impossible for a dog to retrieve one without doing some damage to it. When one is badly shot up, perhaps hit with a full charge of shot at close range, it is even more difficult for the dog to resist the temptation to chew it or perhaps eat it. When my dogs find an immature covey of birds during the early part of hunting season, I prefer to walk away and leave them, and wait until the end of the season when they have reached maturity.

One type of hard-mouthed dog never retrieves a bird. He will pick up every bird he finds, chew it until he is quite positive it is dead, then drop it and resume hunting. I don't have any sinking feelings at all when dealing with a dog of this type, for this is a fault I could never learn to condone. Too many owners are too quick to forgive all faults. I could never bring myself to be so forgiving; I want praise to be meaningful, and I will save the praise for the deserving dog.

Every dog owner should be relentless in his attempt to put an end to the dog's habit of making the bones pop on every bird he retrieves. The dog usually knows he is doing wrong, as evidenced by his actions. With some dogs I get the impression by their no-fear attitude that they're thinking, "So you don't like it? What can you do to stop me?"

Another way to teach the hard-mouthed dog to retrieve tenderly is to place a bird in a wire enclosure of one-inch-mesh chicken wire and let him retrieve it a few times. If he persists in chewing with the bird in the wire enclosure, put a few turns of barbed wire around the chicken wire. When he clamps down on a barb he will be more reluctant to chew. I have worked dogs that would roll the wire enclosure around on the ground until they found a spot where they could get a hold on it without encountering a barb, then retrieve the bundle to hand. These dogs loved to retrieve and were determined to do so, regardless of circumstances!

When the dog first bites down on a bird hard enough to kill it, even though it takes little pressure, that is the time to start to work on him. Don't ignore the first offense in the hope it will be an isolated case, because it will worsen each time the dog retrieves a bird.

It is surprising how many dogs will stop their rough treatment of birds and become tender retrievers if properly corrected each time they commit the offense. All retrieving dogs should be made to handle crippled and dead birds as if they were handling soft-shelled eggs, and have a great fear of damaging them.

Another cure for bird-eating is called the chewing-tobacco cure. This one is for confirmed bird-eaters, and the name tells what it is. I've never used it myself, mainly because chewing tobacco makes me even sicker than bird-eating retrievers do. However, I've been told on very good authority that a wad of chewing tobacco forced down a dog's throat after he has eaten a bird will bring up the bird, the tobacco and anything else on his stomach, and make him never want to think of eating a bird again. I can't fault the theory, anyway.

Pointing and Chasing Rabbits

Many dog owners consider it a serious breach of good manners if their dog points a cottontail rabbit. And if the dog gives half-hearted chase for even ten yards, he is in for serious consequences.

I don't think it's all that bad. One reason is that I have never seen a bird dog (except one that had run loose over an extended period of time and become confirmed in the chasing habit) that would or could chase a rabbit for more than a dozen jumps, for the simple reason that the bird dog is not a trailer. The rabbit always manages to get out of the dog's sight very quickly, and the dog has no way of knowing which way the rabbit went, so the chase is ended. A bird dog usually runs a rabbit by sight only, unless he is a confirmed ground-scenting trailer.

I would pay little attention to a dog that points rabbits. When he realizes you are not interested in them, he may continue to point them, but give him a little gruff talk and let it go at that. In fact, sometimes I encourage a young dog to chase rabbits for a time because it does create interest in hunting and finding game, and this is of the utmost importance to his advancement in training. When it comes time to finish him there is plenty of time to stop him from chasing.

Pointing rabbits is an inherent trait. In the days before the gun was invented the hunter was out for meat for the table, and he would rather have a rabbit than a quail, so he trained the dog to point rabbits as well as quail. Nowadays, field-trial dogs are scored against when they point fur, but I doubt that it is entirely justified.

When quail are not abundant and your dog has scoured the fields for hours without finding birds, it is admittedly quite a letdown to come upon your dog on point with his tail sticking straight up in the air and walk in behind him, fully expecting a large covey to rise, only to see a cottontail rabbit scurry down a rabbit path. But who can say what difference there is between the scent of a rabbit and a quail? (There is some difference, though, of that I am sure, because a bird dog will point with a different stance when on quail, showing much more pronounced style.)

So if your dog does point a rabbit occasionally, don't go into shock. This is the one occasion when the only action you should take is to say, "You had better cut that out," and give him a few gruff words to make him aware that you don't want him to do it again.

Dropping and Sitting Down on Point

At times a dog will drop on point when he crowds a bird by coming upon it totally unexpectedly, perhaps as a result of a sudden shift in the direction of the wind. If the bird is not flushed by the dog's sudden stop, generally this type of dog will then rise on his feet and assume his natural pose on point. However, there are dogs that drop on point and remain on the ground until the birds are flushed and the shooting is over. Of course, this is a throwback to the era when dogs were trained to drop.

The dog that drops and remains on the ground may please the less discriminating owner, but a style-conscious owner would hardly look twice at such a dog. Regretfully, there are too many dog owners who are not interested in a class bird dog. They can get along with any dog if he will point and hold stanchly until they are close enough to get a shot or two before the birds are mere specks on the horizon. It has always been my belief that the majority of owners who are, more or less, satisfied with a dog of this type just don't know how a good dog should perform, and too, perhaps they suffer from the great illusion that shooting birds is the whole measure of the sport to be enjoyed while hunting.

I have seen dogs, admittedly few in number, that would actually sit down when they pointed birds. You would never know, unless well acquainted with the dog, whether the dog was pointing birds or whether he was just resting.

Every man is entitled to his own opinion, but I would find it difficult to be entirely satisfied with just any dog. Moreover, in my view people who settle for second-rate performance in a bird dog usually don't know how good the sport of gunning over dogs can be. Fortunately, the cure for dogs that sit down on point is mostly a question of knowing enough, or caring enough, not to settle for it. If you have a dog that's acquiring the habit of dropping down, not only in unexpected situations but all the time, the best thing to do is to plant some pen-raised birds in your training field, let the dog point them, and then carefully set the dog up on point and stanch him by stroking back of his tail, and setting him back up again every time he drops down.

The Remote-Control Shock Collar

It would be unrealistic to conclude this section on problem solving without dealing with a device capable of dealing with some of the most difficult problems, but incapable of dealing with some easy ones; a device that can yield some of the best results and some of the worst. This device, the remote-control shock collar, is in effect a salvage mechanism for spoiled bird dogs. By its use, the raff of dog society can be converted to the elite merely by pushing a button a time or two. Well—some of the time, anyway.

I sometimes believe the more intelligent dog knows that if you consider him dumb, you are less likely to demand good performance from him. One thing I do know for fact: he couldn't care less what your opinion of him is, as long as it doesn't interfere with his self-styled manner of handling game birds.

The fact that some dogs are too smart to cope with is why some dog owners get poor performance from their dogs. But it doesn't have to be this way.

As an illustration, take the dog that is a self-hunter. He doesn't want you to observe what he does because he wants to perform in a manner of his own choosing. Your whistle is his timepiece—it tells him how long he can run out of control without missing his ride back to the kennel. When in despair you stop blowing the whistle he knows you have given up on him, so up he pops, seemingly out of nowhere. At no time was he as far from you as you imagined; he knew where you were every minute of his absence, but didn't care.

He grins at you, wags his tail in a most

friendly fashion and hopes you believe he has been looking for you. You are so glad to see him your spirits, which had been at low ebb, soar to new heights—what a nightmare the poor dog must have suffered, all the while he was looking for you! You may not believe it, but already the lost dog is looking for an opportune moment to become lost again.

Using the same dog, let's change his nonsensical manner of performance. Rent or purchase a remote-control shock unit, and put the collar on him. As he vanishes over the hill, give him a long blast on the whistle and at the same time, give him a jolt of current of one or two seconds' duration. Too much shock should not be used until you see the result of a mild shock. His scream of "Help!" will tell you when to release the control button. Obviously, you shouldn't use the unit indiscriminately, or you may make a plodder of a potentially good dog; you don't want to take chances of destroying his good qualities.

However, when you observe the result from one blast of your whistle plus the reaction to the shock, you will realize you have been wasting a lot of time just hoping to get his attention. From this point on you will have his undivided attention; he will be at your side, not when he feels like it, but *now*—the instant you press the button on the transmitter. Small oak sprouts, buckbrush, and tall grass may be disturbed by the backwash of air from his haste to get to you for protection from what he doesn't know. You will realize that your fears over his poor hearing were unfounded. He will suddenly have no difficulty in hearing and understanding the meaning of the word "Whoa," a word which had no meaning to him before the shock.

I don't mean to sound facetious, for the remote-control shock unit is not a toy to be playfully tested on your dog, nor is it a cure-all. It should probably never be used on dogs of retiring disposition. It will not make a close-hunting dog hunt a wider pattern, but it will alter the wide dog's hunting pattern and cause him to hunt to the gun.

Never use it on a dog for the sake of testing his reaction to the shock. Use it sparingly and then only to achieve results in correcting faults which punishment has failed to correct. But you will find its use indispensable on dogs with an adamant disposition.

After the initial shock, give the dog sufficient time to reform. It isn't likely, but if he disregards the lesson, give him another, allowing time between shocks for him to ponder his dilemma. Don't expect to cure a dog completely of an ingrained fault in one day, though even the dog with a churlish disposition will make instant change in his manner of doing the job when he realizes he has no alternative.

Every professional trainer should own a remote-control shock unit, for it reduces mammoth problems to simplicity. A big point in its favor: the dog never associates the shock with the trainer; he always considers his trainer as his protector from the dreaded shock. Thus you should be careful never to use a shock unit on a strange dog—if you do, you may lose both the dog and the collar unit. If the dog doesn't know you, he will not come to you for protection, and you may find him many days later and many miles distant, if at all. If a dog doesn't have at least a modicum of affection for you, he will bolt. So don't say I didn't warn you.

Do not shock a dog unless he is in the act of misbehaving. It would serve no purpose and would surely do harm. Make sure the dog can take punishment before using the unit on him; never use it on a dog of shy temperament, because it will not overcome shyness but can conceivably cause shyness, if used improperly.

Do not shock the dog for pointing rabbits, stink birds, terrapins, or meadowlarks. In fact, never shock the dog while he is on point; it might make him bird-shy.

Release the transmitter button at the very first cry. A sustained shock is unnecessary, even for the most obstinate dog.

Do shock him for intentionally flushing birds, however, and do shock him for chasing farm animals. If he is permitted to chase farm animals, you have lost another hunting area. If you shock him for mutilating birds, unless he has great desire, he will refuse to retrieve. Shock him for refusal to honor another dog. Shock him for ignoring the whistle, making sure he is not on point.

When he will hunt to the gun and becomes

controllable, remove the collar unit and re-place it with the dummy collar, as a reminder of what happened and what could happen again. Hopefully, he won't need more re-minding.

The remote-control shock unit is not, I re-peat, a panacea—it doesn't solve all problems, and it doesn't suit all dogs—but what it does do can be close to miraculous on occasion, and that is, to take dogs from the bottom rung of dog society and put them back on the top. If you use it intelligently, it can transform dogs that are as useless as rocks in a potato patch back into useful citizens again, quicker and better than any way I know.

V

Appendix

Force-Breaking to Retrieve

Force-breaking a dog to retrieve is a time-consuming job. It doesn't take much time daily, but the training must extend over a lengthy period. However, it is absolutely positive if done right.

To prepare objects to retrieve, cut three sections from an ax handle, about eight inches each in length. On the first section, tack strips of tin for its entire length. On the second section, drill two small holes through each end and drive heavy nails through them so that they form an X. (The wood will probably split if the holes are not first drilled.) This makes a sawbuck which raises the section a few inches off the ground. Leave the third section plain, as is.

Select a place, preferably inside a building where there will be nothing to distract the dog's attention. Take the dog's left paw in your left hand, if you are right-handed, and exert pressure. This will cause him to open his mouth. Place the plain section in the dog's mouth, holding his jaws closed by placing your hand underneath his jaw. Force him to hold the section for a few minutes. When you are ready for him to release it, give him the command "Give." He will be glad to give it to you on command because he doesn't want to hold it anyhow. Again put pressure on his paw, and say, "Open." When he opens his mouth immediately clap the section in his mouth again, and say, "Hold." Repeat this procedure until he will take the section in his mouth without applying pressure to his foot, and will release it upon the command "Give."

Inspect the plain section to see if there are teeth marks on it. If there are, switch to the section with the strips of tin attached to it, and use this section for a time. He will not bite down on it but will be more reluctant to take it in his mouth and glad to release it. He does not like to have metal touch his teeth.

When he opens his mouth on the command "Open," and will hold the section in his

Force-breaking a dog to retrieve. The nails in the end of the dummy hold it up off the ground and make it easier to pick up.

mouth at the command "Hold," and release it at the command "Give," then hold the section in front of him where he will be forced to take a step to take it in his mouth. When he steps out and takes the section in his mouth, increase the distance and the number of steps he must take each time. When he will take four or five steps to take the buck in his mouth, then it is time to switch to the sawbuck.

Throw the buck a few feet and command him, "Dead bird, fetch," and see if he will scoop it up and fetch it to you. The nails which you have driven through to form the sawbuck will allow him to get his jaw under the section.

There you have it. All you need do is continue the training until he will retrieve the buck every time you throw it. With perseverance, you will have a foolproof retriever, force-broken to retrieve on command, whether he wants to or not.

Making a Quail Comeback Pen

Every bird-dog trainer or owner who has one or more bird dogs to train should construct and use a quail comeback pen. If used only occasionally, it is the ideal training set-up. With its use, it will not be necessary to tramp the fields day after day and chance finding birds. You *know* you will have birds to work your dog. When you want to do some training or would just like to see your favorite

The quail comeback pen. Boards are piled on top to discourage birds from flying into the wire and scalping themselves.

dog work, all you need do is release some birds and you are in business. Even though your dog may need no work, you will enjoy seeing him work, and he will enjoy the work even more. A dog's daily routine in the kennel becomes filled with boredom if he is never taken afield between hunting seasons. The use of pen-reared quail has no equal in the training of bird dogs.

The pen should be constructed of one-inch-thick pine or oak lumber, or if you want it more sturdy, you can use two-by-twos. The pen should be eight feet long, three feet wide and no more than twelve inches high. (Some instructions recommend eighteen inches as a height, but the additional six inches serve no useful purpose—the quail cannot walk on it, and it permits the birds to fly against the wire on top with more force, making them more likely to scalp themselves.)

Both sides and the bottom of the pen should be covered with half-inch hardware cloth. Both ends should be solid board construction, with one end hinged for release of the birds. Wire should be used for the top, but boards should be available to lay across the top during the dark hours to keep dogs and predators from mashing the wire down.

The passage by which the quail return to the pen is made of one-inch mesh poultry wire, rolled into a funnel. The funnel should extend into the cage approximately twelve inches. The large end of the funnel should be about eight inches wide to enable the quail to see the opening, and should taper to four inches.

The funnel must slope upward on the inside of the pen and should be higher than the eye level of a quail. Fasten the wire at a point near the top of the cage with a short piece of wire. This will prevent the funnel from sagging with the weight of the birds as they return to the pen. (If not wired in this manner, in time the funnel will sag to a point below the eye level of the quail and they will find their way out of the pen.)

The four-inch hole at the small end of the funnel is large enough for the quail to pass through on the return to the cage, but too small for all but the very smallest varmints to enter. Even so, just one very small opossum, wanton killers that they are, will slaughter every bird in the cage should you become careless and fail to close the entrance after the birds have returned to the pen.

Return holes on both sides of the pen are better than using one side only. If there is only one hole and some of the quail happen to get on the side where there is no hole, they may walk up and down on that side of the pen for some time looking for the hole, greatly increasing their chances of being taken by a predator.

A one-pound coffee can inserted into the return hole in the funnel with a stick run through the wire in front of the can will keep varmints from dislodging the can and gaining entrance to the pen during the night.

The first time the birds are released, it is best not to do any training that day. Let the quail birds walk out of the pen at their leisure and they will not stray far and will find their way back with no difficulty. If they are flushed several times and driven a considerable distance from the pen before they become familiar with their surroundings, they may have difficulty in finding their way back to the pen.

The first few times the birds are released, it is a good idea to leave a bird or two in the pen as an inducement to the other birds to return. In a week or so it is safe to release the entire bunch if necessary.

Pen-reared quail purchased from some sources are better at returning to the cage than others, depending upon whether they were raised in a building or in the open in pens. If raised in a building, they seem to want to return to a building.

During the training sessions, the birds will be flushed repeatedly and you will hear very few whistles from them. They covey again by talking to each other in nearly inaudible cheeps and chirps. In the summer months when the cover is green and dense, and the mating season is at the peak, they lose much of their caution.

A quail call is a very effective means of inducing the released birds to start calling to each other.

When reared in captivity, quail will be poor flyers for a while, but after they have been released a dozen times and have had the opportunity to condition their wing muscles, you will be unable to distinguish between them and wild birds. It is amazing how quickly they learn to avoid obstacles when in flight, such as wire fences.

The first few times quail are released, when the ground cover is sparse, they will do a lot of running. This provides many chances for the young dog to point them. When the dog can see them running, and will make numerous points without trying to catch the birds, one can get in a lot of work and the training mission can be accomplished in a much shorter time.

The number of quail to be purchased will depend upon the number of dogs to be worked. Twenty quail for each pen is about the right number. Never release the quail in a single group if you can prevent it. At times they may come out of the pen so fast that they are all out before you can get the release gate closed. They will then fly as a group, and may take refuge in a brush pile or other inaccessible place. When released one at a time, however, they will run and hide, thus offering more opportunities for single bird point, enabling you to get more work done.

Twenty quail will drink about one pint of water each day in hot weather. Two cups of turkey grower is about all they will eat in one day. When fed turkey grower they have no need for grit to help in the digestion of food, but they must have access to a dust bath to remain free of mites. I have seen quail in captivity starve to death when offered whole grain corn and milo in the feed. They had never seen corn or milo and had no idea it was their natural food.

When quail are released for stocking an area, they must be fed the same feed they have been accustomed to until they learn to eat the lespedeza seed, acorns and other wild seed they normally eat when reared in the wild.

Water must be available to them near their release site until they learn where to go for water. If food and water is not available to them near the release site, all stockings are time and money wasted.

Finally, note that your state law may require anyone holding game birds in captivity to have a permit. Contact your state fish and game department to verify the requirements in your area.

Using the Quail Harness

When the area the trainer has to work in is too restricted to permit effective use of the come-back pen, he may make do quite satisfactorily by employing a quail harness. This is a comparatively new product which, as the name implies, is used with a live pen-raised quail. The live bird will hold the dog's interest long after his interest in a dead object, such as a quail wing, has waned. Even so, it is a good idea to limit lessons to relatively short

periods of time; fifteen minutes daily is sufficient.

In use, the live bird is placed in the
harness, and this in turn is tied to about fifteen feet of line and a short pole like a fishing
pole. With this arrangement the trainer can
exert complete control over the quail and, to a
great extent, the dog as well. He can "flush"
the bird very easily by quickly lifting the pole
at the precise moment when he wants the
bird flushed.

The harnessed quail has quite a bit of
freedom, being able to run the distance of the
pole and line, which is twenty feet or so. The
bird can thus run and hide, requiring the dog
to use his nose to locate it.

When the trainer starts working the un-
trained dog, it is best to use a check cord. The
dog must learn, first of all, that you are capable of controlling him; that he must obey
all commands without hesitation. Of course,
these commands are taught as his training
progresses.

After the dog has progressed in training to
the point where the check cord can be removed, he is likely to try flushing and
chasing, but he can do little chasing because
the range of the bird is restricted to the length
of the pole and line. This makes the problem
of catching the dog effortless; it is easy to take
the dog back to the exact spot where he mis-
behaved, to pose him on point, to talk to him
and pet him and, if he continues to break of
his own accord or at flush, to give him a few

gentle reminders of what to expect when he does wrong. By constant control over the dog for a period of one or two months, and by use of light punishment each time he commits misbehavior, he will learn the trainer will not tolerate misbehavior and your training problem is under control.

The use of a harnessed quail makes teaching a dog to honor a relatively simple task. With both dogs under control with a check cord there is no way to refuse to stop on command or to go ahead of the pointing dog and steal the point. Some dogs will honor at the first opportunity; some must be taught what to do when they see a dog on point. Others may refuse to honor because of jealousy, and some may be short on brains.

One other point in favor of the quail harness: The spikes on the leather harness are sharp enough to make a dog think twice about biting down hard on the bird while in the process of retrieving.

Kennel Sanitation

One gallon of stock dip mixed with fifty gallons of water makes an excellent solution to keep dogs free of skin irritation and to kill such vermin as fleas, ticks, and mites. It also discourages flies from biting the dog.

Pour the stock dip in a fifty-gallon oil drum and fill it with water. Dip the dog once a week. It will rid the dog of his doggy smell, wash away dead hair, and keep his coat in a healthy condition.

This solution is also excellent for washing down the kennel floors. Wet the runs, let it stand for a few minutes, and then hose it down with water. This makes a clean, sanitary kennel, eliminates objectionable kennel odors, and eliminates the possibility of flies breeding in the kennels.

A Cheap Positive Mange Cure

Mange has always been a serious health problem for dogs of all ages. Forty or fifty years ago, a sure cure was not to be found. Today, there are many treatments, some very effective, some not so dependable.

Many dog owners have the mistaken belief that used motor oil will cure mange. Used oil is a messy treatment which remains on the dog's coat for weeks, and it has no curative power. Without doubt, however, it does help to relieve the itch, hence less scratching, and as a result, it does retard the mange for a short time.

Many cases diagnosed by the home veterinarian as mange are nothing more than skin irritation, possibly caused by shredded bedding. Oat straw is the worst choice of bedding because of its shredding tendencies. Small pieces become lodged in the dog's hair, causing him to scratch, which causes more irritation. Fleas will cause a dog to scratch and his skin will become irritated to such an extent the owner will be convinced the dog has mange.

The following recipe will definitely cure all types of mange, including the dreaded red mange, the most difficult to cure. (If it fails to effect a speedy cure, the dog does not, in fact, have mange.)

One pound of pure lard (not vegetable short-ening)
One pound of clear petroleum jelly
One pint of unused motor oil
One pint of kerosene
Two ounces of carbolic acid
One ounce of Creolin (to discourage the dog from licking)
Sufficient sulphur to make a creamy paste which is easy to rub into the dog's skin

To eliminate the possibility of a fire in the home, these ingredients must be boiled out-doors, over an open flame. Use a container with a tight-fitting lid to keep the flame from the highly inflammable liquids.

Place the container on the flame, put the lard and petroleum jelly in and allow it to melt. Remove the container from the flame and add the oil and kerosene. Be very careful from this point on. Place the container on the flame once more and bring the contents to a rolling boil. Remove it from the flame and allow the mixture to cool. After an hour or so, add the Creolin, carbolic acid and sulphur.

Although not essential to the effectiveness of the cure, it helps to effect the cure some-what more rapidly if the dog is bathed before the mixture is applied to his skin.

The mixture should be applied to the dog's entire body, and worked well into the skin, especially to the parts that are red and raw. All scabs should be removed so that the medication can get to the skin. Where the greatest amount of irritation shows, do a thorough job of rubbing the mixture in. Spend some time on the application, because unlike many remedies, one application will do such a thorough job, there will be no need to apply the second one.

If red spots remain after ten days, touch up the spots to make certain it will not break out again.

If, after the touch-up application, the skin does not become healthy and the red spots do not permanently disappear, there is every liklihood the dog did not have mange, but perhaps a blood disease.

New hair will appear in a short time and the dog will stop itching and scratching immediately after the one application of the mixture.

Whelping Quarters

The following may seem of relatively minor importance to those who have had experience in raising a litter of puppies, but it can mean the difference in raising all of a litter or none.

The shape of the whelping house is of vital importance for the safety of the puppies. A fifty-gallon barrel makes an ideal house for any dog, except dams at whelping time, for then its dog-shaped contour leaves the puppies no avenue of escape when the dam lies down, and she may crush them with her body weight.

The whelping quarters should be no larger than necessary so the puppies cannot get too far from the dam. Also, the smaller the house the less body heat will be required to heat it during the winter months.

The dam should have a clean bed of hay or grass when the time comes for her to deliver. Never use an excess of bedding, lest the puppies get under the bedding and become lost from the dam; not knowing where they are, she may lie on them. The old bedding should be removed and replaced with fresh, clean bedding after the dam has become adjusted after whelping.

The opening to the quarters should be high enough for the puppies to be unable to get out of the house until they are old enough to walk and climb back into the house without assistance. Otherwise, should one or more get out of the house on a very cold night, their survival will depend on whether the dam will help them back in the house. And while some will, some won't. However, don't have the entrance to the house so high that the dam will bruise her udders when entering or leaving.

Not all dams are good mothers. Some of them want very little to do with their puppies, and during warm weather, will visit them only when necessary to feed them.

Care of the Dam at Whelping Time

Select a secluded section of the kennel for the dam when it is time for her to whelp. She will be more contented if located away from other dogs; if located in a kennel next to another dog, she will be fearful the dog may harm her puppies and she may destroy them in order to protect them. This is illogical on the dam's part, but nevertheless it does happen.

Never interfere with the dam at whelping time. It is best not to go near her once you are satisfied she is in no whelping difficulty. Do not handle the puppies until she is over her nervous state, which may last a week or more. Everyone will be anxious to see the puppies, but as long as they don't cry, you can be sure they are healthy and receiving the proper amount of nourishment. If anything is wrong they will tell you about it with their constant crying.

Once you are satisfied they are contented, wait a week before you take them out of the house to count the males and females, note their coloring, and inspect them for malformation.

When they are old enough to get out of the house by themselves, they must be kept far enough from other dogs so that it is impossible for them to come in contact with each other. If a dog bites them they are certain to incur lacerations that will become infected. Puppies are much more susceptible to infection than mature dogs. A four-inch welded wire between kennels will not prevent dogs from biting each other through the wire. When building a kennel one should use a two-by-two-inch welded wire or chain-link wire.

The dam knows what is best for her puppies, so let her care for them in her own fashion. If there is silence in the whelping quarters, all is well. You can be assured that the puppies are warm and their stomachs are full.

A Word about the Professional Trainer

Every bird-dog trainer has reluctantly worked dogs which did not have the slightest chance of ever amounting to anything worthwhile. If you are honest and tell the owner his dog isn't making progress, you sometimes have an irate customer to deal with. You must be truthful and aboveboard with all customers regardless of whose hackle gets ruffled, though if you come out flat and tell the owner his dog will make someone a good pet, you have said too much.

Owners who send their dog to the professional trainer should make certain he has selected a trainer with experience and is capable. A trainer without experience can kill a good prospect's potential. Once lost, through ignorance of the proper procedure in training a dog, good qualities are hard to restore.

When the trainer has finished your dog's training, ask to be shown how the dog performs. Find out if he will point stanchly, retrieve and honor. The trainer, if he has earned his money, will be glad to show you what an improved dog you now own. No trainer wants unjustified criticism.

When you take your dog hunting it is your duty to the dog, the trainer and to yourself not to let the dog ignore his training. There are many that will if you permit it. Handle the dog properly; be unrelenting in your demands. Ask him to perform for you just as well as he did for the trainer. He will do it if you don't ignore or make excuses for a single miscue.

You have seen your dog perform in good fashion, you know he knows how it should be done. If you allow him to misbehave, admit that it is your fault. The trainer must not be criticized for your lack of determination to make the dog perform as you have seen him perform. He has devoted many hours to training your dog and has given the dog his best training effort. By and large, dog owners get full value received from competent trainers. Don't let the trainer's effort be without reward.

If the reader of this book has learned the lesson contained in the following words, I will consider myself rewarded: "Handle your dog or he will surely handle you."

INDEX